ROCKHOUNDING

Delaware, Maryland, and the Washington, DC Metro Area

Help Us Keep This Guide Up to Date

Every effort has been made by the author and editors to make this guide as accurate and useful as possible. However, many things can change after a guide is published—roads are detoured, phone numbers change, facilities come under new management, etc.

We would appreciate hearing from you concerning your experiences with this guide and how you feel it could be improved and kept up to date. While we may not be able to respond to all comments and suggestions, we'll take them to heart, and we'll also make certain to share them with the author. Please send your comments and suggestions to the following address:

FalconGuides
Reader Response/Editorial Department
246 Goose Lane
Guilford, CT 06437

Or you may e-mail us at: editorial@falcon.com

Thanks for your input, and happy rockhounding!

ROCKHOUNDING
Delaware, Maryland, and the Washington, DC Metro Area

A Guide to the Areas' Best Rockhounding Sites

ROBERT BEARD

GUILFORD, CONNECTICUT
HELENA, MONTANA

FALCONGUIDES®

An imprint of Rowman & Littlefield
Falcon, FalconGuides, and Outfit Your Mind are registered trademarks of Rowman & Littlefield.

Distributed by NATIONAL BOOK NETWORK

British Library Cataloguing-in-Publication Information Available

Library of Congress Cataloging-in-Publication Data

Beard, Robert D.
Rockhounding Delaware, Maryland, and the Washington, DC metro area : a guide to the areas' best rockhounding sites / Robert Beard.
pages cm
Includes bibliographical references and index.
ISBN 978-1-4930-0336-5 (pbk.) — ISBN 978-1-4930-1496-5 (e-book) 1. Rocks—Collection and preservation—Delaware—Guidebooks. 2. Rocks—Collection and preservation—Maryland—Guidebooks. 3. Rocks—Collection and preservation—Washington (D.C.)—Guidebooks. 4. Minerals—Collection and preservation—New York (State)—Guidebooks. 5. Delaware—Guidebooks. 6. Maryland—Guidebooks. 7. Washington (D.C.)—Guidebooks. I. Title. II. Title: Rock hounding Delaware, Maryland, and the Washington, DC metro area.
QE445.D4B43 2015
557.5—dc23

2015001889

The author and Rowman & Littlefield assume no liability for accidents happening to, or injuries sustained by, readers who engage in the activities described in this book.

This book is dedicated to my wife, Rosalina; my son, Daniel; my daughter, Roberta; and our other family members and friends who came on field trips with us. Your support and inspiration made this book possible.

CONTENTS

Physiographic Provinces of Maryland and Delaware

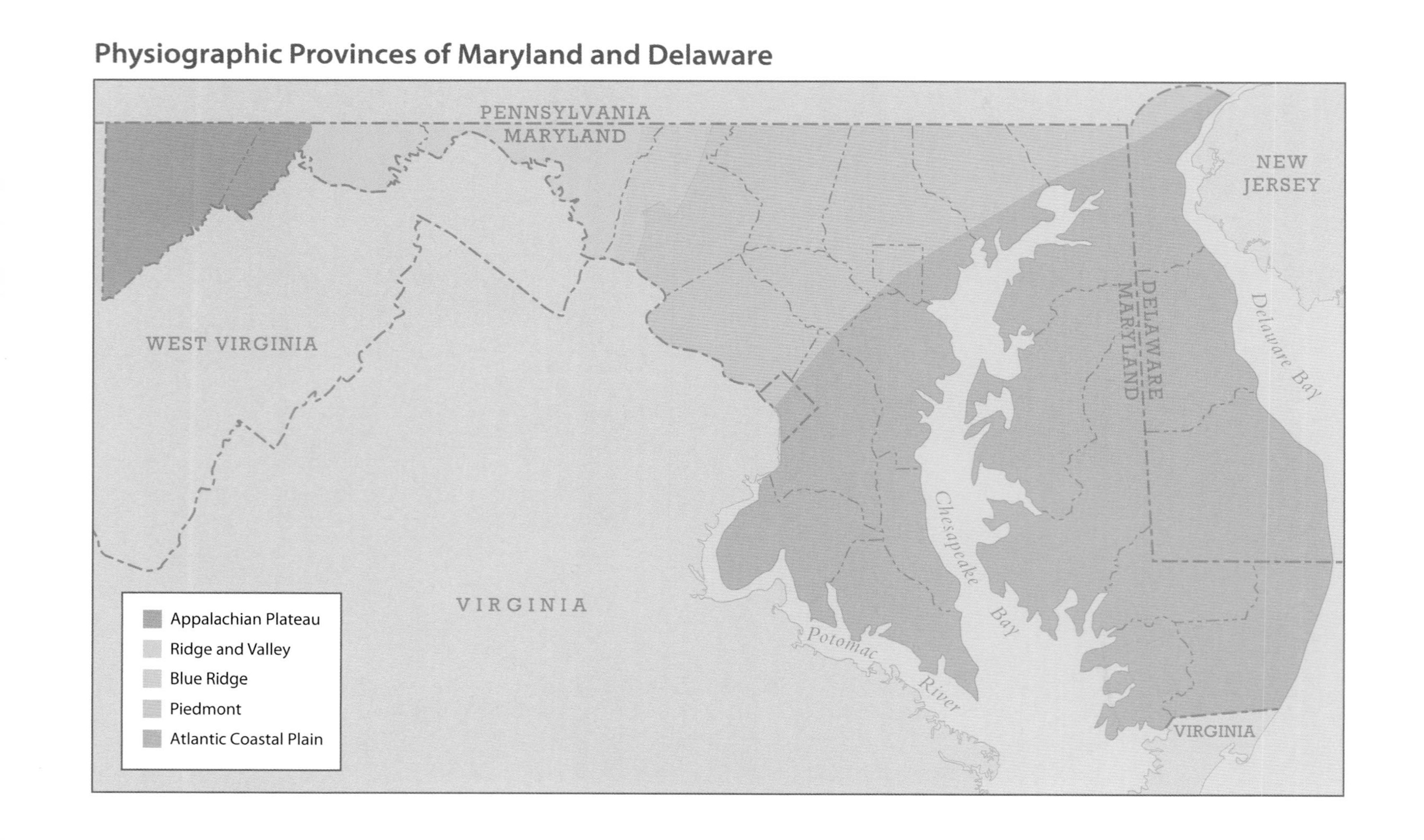

Washington, DC Metropolitan Area

ACKNOWLEDGMENTS

Many people have helped make this book possible. I would first like to thank my editor at *Rock & Gem* magazine, Lynn Varon, who put me in contact with Globe Pequot Press, and William Kappele, another Rockhounding series writer and contributing editor at *Rock & Gem*, who suggested me to Lynn as a potential author for Globe Pequot in 2011. My writing experience with *Rock & Gem* has greatly expanded my capabilities as a geologist and has been a great asset to my career.

I would like to thank my editors at Globe Pequot, David Legere and Meredith Dias, for their encouragement and support for the book, and Melissa Baker in the map department, who gave me extremely helpful comments and suggestions. Thanks are also due to the production staff and the many people who were instrumental in producing and distributing the book.

In the course of this work, I had very useful discussions with university professors, mining industry personnel, state geologists, and experienced collectors that I met in the field. I greatly appreciated the ideas and discussions that I had with Frank Pazzaglia, Johnny Johnson, Steve Stokowski, Bill Kochanov, Priscilla Carol, and Ron Tonucci, among many others.

While doing research for this book, I came across many websites, blogs, newsletters, and forums that gave excellent information on potential sites and often provided key information that enabled me to find difficult-to-locate sites. I really appreciated the writings of Jeff Nagel, Ken Casey, Gene Hartstein, John Need, Anne Province, and John Betts, along with the Delaware Valley Earth Science Society (DVESS); the Baltimore Mineral Society; the Gem, Lapidary and Mineral Society of Washington, DC; and the Northern Virginia Mineral Club. I also appreciated all the support that my friends from the Central Pennsylvania Rock and Mineral Club gave when they learned that I was working on this book.

State agency resources included the Delaware Geological Survey, the Maryland Department of Natural Resources, the Maryland Geological Survey, and the Virginia Department of Mines, Minerals and Energy. Their websites, online guidebooks, and conference proceedings all provided valuable information.

Lastly, I would like to thank my wife, Rosalina; my son, Daniel; and my daughter, Roberta. During the research for this book, they came with me on several trips, as did my sister-in-law, Maria Tellez, and our friend Valerie Gray. We had the opportunity to make several of these trips during the summer months when the weather was good, and found that Delaware, Maryland, and Washington, DC, offer some of the best field trips to be found anywhere. I hope that you, your friends, and your families use this guide to find good field trips that become among your most memorable experiences.

INTRODUCTION

But this is an example of an underlying principle to mineral collecting: even ordinary people will recognize extraordinary mineral occurrences and will preserve specimens, if only as a curiosity.

—John Betts, 2009

This book is geared toward that rockhound or geologist who wants to visit sites without advance arrangements. Virtually every type of rockhounding trip can be found in this book. Some sites will allow you to park and pick up rocks as soon as you get out of your car. Other sites require some walking, and some sites require strenuous hiking over bad terrain. Some sites do not allow rock collecting at all, but are still worth visiting. At some sites you will likely find lots of minerals or fossils, and at others you may have to work hard to find anything. I have done my best to help you easily find these sites and let you know what to expect.

Delaware, Maryland, and the area around Washington, DC, are among the most historic parts of the United States. The region has some of the first mines and quarries that were developed in the nation. Many of these mines are all but forgotten and either developed, posted, or turned into parkland. While the region has a wide variety of mineral occurrences, as in much of the East, many of these are on private land or are public sites where mineral collecting is prohibited. Some of the public sites that used to be open for collecting have also become national monuments, and collecting there now is strictly forbidden. However, the good news is that these sites are generally open to public access, which still is better than a private site that is not open to the public.

In this book I have focused on identifying sites that you can visit by yourself or with your family without significant advance planning or permission. I have personally checked every one of the sites in this book. Many of the sites are roadcuts or outcrops that are somewhat limited in size but are reasonably accessible to visitors. Roadcuts are often within the highway right-of-way and sometimes belong to the state or local government. Generally you can collect in these areas if they are safe, not disrupting traffic, and clearly not marked against entry. For what it is worth, I have never had a problem with collecting at roadcuts, but I always make certain that I am not inside posted ground and that I am not in an area where I am posing a risk to traffic.

Interstate highways are illegal collecting sites, and I am aware of some mineral occurrences along Maryland interstates that are referenced in other texts that I kept out of this guide for that reason. There are few feelings that are more discouraging than being at a site and having a police car pull up behind you, especially if you know you are not supposed to be there. Of course, land and access status can change at any time. Even if a private site is not posted, this guide does not imply or suggest that collecting at the site is permitted.

Many entries in this book are in county parks, state forests, state parks, federal lands, or other places that are accessible to the public, and while you can go to these sites, rock collecting is prohibited in many of them. A noticeable exception is shark teeth collecting along Maryland and Virginia beaches, and this is generally allowed in state parks. However, rock-collecting rules are not applied uniformly in many cases. If you look at the park regulations, you will generally find that any form of ground disturbance, which technically includes simply picking up a rock, is strictly prohibited.

However, many of these same parks and state agencies publish field guides to these parks. In these cases you will have to use your best judgment as to whether or not to collect rocks if you visit a site. If there are signs clearly stating "no mineral collecting," do not collect rocks. Likewise, if you are in a place where you know collecting is forbidden, you can look at the rocks, but do not collect them. Nearly all state parks, while offering excellent access to see former mines, quarries, and outcrops, do not allow any collecting. Where an interesting mineral or fossil occurrence is on publicly accessible land but collecting is prohibited, I have still listed it in this book if I have visited it and consider the locality worthy of a visit by anyone interested in rocks. I have not yet found a site where it is against the law to look at the rocks.

Delaware, Maryland, and the DC area do not have many fee-collecting sites, which is unfortunate, as these are generally very good places for collectors and are well worth visiting. However, it is worth noting that many of the shark teeth beaches collect a fee for parking, and the state parks generally charge a fee to enter the park, so in a way these might be considered fee sites.

I have stayed away from listing mine and quarry sites where you have to obtain advance permission and appointments, as many rockhounds often do not have the ability to schedule and make advance arrangements. Quarries and mines are generally best visited as a group with a local mineral club or other organization. Such group trips to quarries could be well worth your time, as you'll bypass identifying landowners and permission issues, but you must also make sure that you bring your own hard hat, steel-toed boots, hammer, and other tools that might be appropriate for the rock types you may encounter. Active quarries in Delaware, Maryland, and the DC area make great collecting sites when you can get in, but unfortunately many of the quarries are under new ownership and no longer allow mineral collecting.

For the rockhound with family members who don't love rocks quite as much as you do, this book also includes local attractions near each site. Many of these are local state parks, nearby lakes, and, in urban settings, nearby malls and cities. These should help you plan a trip that's fun for everyone.

Delaware, Maryland, and Washington, DC, span a wide area, and it is nearly impossible to cover every locality. While I attempted to include as many sites as possible in this book, I found that the list of good sites kept growing, and eventually I had to draw the line on adding localities. The good news is that the more I kept looking, the more sites I kept finding. This is important, as it shows that there are still more sites to visit. I have never run out of new places to find rocks.

The best way to learn about rock collecting is to go out and look for rocks. You and your companions are bound to see some interesting geology and scenery too as you experience the adventure of going on a field trip, even if just for a morning or afternoon.

ROCKHOUNDING BASICS

[The observer] need not burden himself with accoutrements. A hammer, pretty stout in its dimensions, with a round blunt face and a flat sharp tail; a note-book and a good pocket-lens, are all he needs to begin with.

—Sir Archibald Geikie, 1858

COLLECTING EQUIPMENT

Rockhounding can be a low-budget hobby, especially when you are just starting out, as the entry requirements are relatively minimal. Literally all you need are your eyes and hands to see and pick up interesting rocks. However, as you advance you'll want some additional tools.

A good **hammer** is the most important tool for the rockhound. I recommend a rock pick hammer with a pointed tip. Hardware stores don't usually carry these, but they are available at some surveying supply shops, at rock shows, and online. My preferred brand is an Estwing foot-long hammer with a pointed tip and a Shock Reduction Grip. I have used mine for over thirty years. It is almost impossible to destroy, despite thousands of whacks against very hard rocks and lots of time outside in the rain and snow. Do not use a regular claw hammer. These will break apart quickly, and the steel that shoots off the hammer head when it hits a rock can be very dangerous.

If you are hammering, it is also critical to wear **safety glasses or goggles.** I wear glasses normally to see, and my glasses have often been damaged by flying rock chips and steel. In the event that I am hammering large rocks on a constant basis, such as in a quarry, I will cover my glasses with safety goggles. When collecting in urban environments, rocks are often associated with broken glass, which becomes another hazard when hit with a hammer.

I also use a **chisel** to help break apart rocks when needed, but many chisels have very wide blades and are difficult to use when splitting the soft, finely bedded sediments that are common in many fossiliferous shales. I sometimes use a cheap **flat-bladed screwdriver** for soft shaly rocks where a chisel is too big to use. I know this is not the proper use of a screwdriver, but I have not found a better tool for splitting apart soft shaly rocks. Of course, if you try to use a flat-bladed screwdriver to split apart hard rocks, you really are then abusing the tool and run the risk of breaking the screwdriver or injuring yourself. In a case where you are splitting harder rocks, your best tool will likely be a chisel, and you may need to find one with a very narrow blade if the rocks must be split along very tight fractures.

Gloves are the next critical item. In the old days I used to do fieldwork without gloves, but realized quickly that it was a dangerous practice. Make sure you protect your hands. All of us with day jobs that involve a computer are in big trouble if we temporarily lose the use of a finger or hand. Get a good pair of heavy leather work gloves from your local hardware or big-box store. You will also find that gloves are great when moving through briars, climbing on sharp rocks, and avoiding broken glass. It is also extremely easy to pinch your bare fingers when moving around large rocks, but gloves will help prevent this. It is better to get the end of your glove caught under a rock than the tip of your finger.

Get a good pair of steel-toed or equivalent **boots** to protect your feet. Having steel-toed boots is a requirement for collecting in quarries and mines, and it is very easy to find and purchase a good pair. I prefer to have relatively lightweight boots. Be sure to walk in them before purchasing to find a pair that fits comfortably.

A **hard hat,** while not needed for collecting at most roadcuts or places without overhead hazards, is equipment you should always have readily available. While you may not need one for casual rock collecting, you should have one with you or in your car in case you get invited to collect in a quarry or visit an active mine.

A **field book** and **camera** are also very useful for recording key site information. I like to record coordinates of sites and take notes of what I have found for future reference. I also use a small pocket-size digital camera and often take hundreds of shots a day to increase my chances of getting that perfect shot. A **hand lens** to inspect mineral and fossils up close is also very useful. I recommend getting a quality hand lens that is at least 10X magnification.

Carrying your rocks from the site is often a chore. I like to use a small **backpack** when I have to walk a long distance, but sometimes a five-gallon plastic bucket works best. A bucket is useful when you are picking up muddy rocks, and it is easy to put in your car. Just be careful not to break the bottom of the bucket if you intend to also use it for water. I have ruined several buckets with large, sharp rocks.

A **wagon** is good to have if you are working in quarries or places where you can expect to take out significant amounts of rocks. If you go on a trip with a mineral club to a quarry, you can always tell who knows what they are doing, as they often come with a wagon to haul the rocks out of the pit. Collecting lots of rocks in a quarry is fine, as what you do not collect is just going to go to a crusher. However, do not take your wagon to a roadcut. If you have reached this stage of rock collecting, you probably already know that you are collecting too many rocks. Taking a wagon to a roadcut may also attract attention from the police. No further explanation needed here.

GPS UNITS AND MAPS

Before digital mapping, I used to find every site by using topographic and highway maps, but those days are long over. I now use a handheld **Global Positioning System (GPS) unit** to record key site location information, and I use the coordinate feature on my car GPS to take me to the site. I still meet people who are not using all available features of their GPS unit, such as the latitude and longitude feature, so be sure you brush up on all the available features of yours.

Many rockhounds don't have this dedicated device, but rather use their smartphone GPS app. My GPS is still separate from my phone, and I like to record my locations by hand. However, I have used a smartphone in the field and found the satellite imagery, combined with real-time tracking, was very helpful for finding difficult-to-locate sites. If you do not use a GPS at all, I strongly recommend that you start, either with a dedicated device or an app. Keep up with advances in mapping technology too, as newer and better navigation methods will likely keep coming.

Despite the advantages of GPS units and smartphones, you should always have **maps** as a backup. I like to have a state map, and I often get free maps at rest areas. I have also found my standard US road atlas works very well. Batteries can die, and satellite and mobile signals can be dropped in wilderness and urban areas where you do not have good clearance for satellite signals. Sometimes your charger will also short out, which happened to me on a multiday collecting trip, and I suddenly felt like I was traveling blind. A good highway map can also be a relatively simple check for your GPS unit.

If possible, you should also get **topographic maps** of your site. I used to buy hard-copy maps, but they are expensive, especially when you are looking at several sites. I recently bought a set of topographic maps on CDs from National Geographic, but unfortunately they have discontinued the CD series and replaced them with online maps. I found these to be completely unsuitable for my purposes, as I am often in areas without Internet access. I am hoping that technology and Internet access will improve to the point where I will access online topographic maps, but for now I am still working with my older copies on CD.

HEALTH AND SAFETY

Rockhounding presents many hazards that you will not encounter in other hobbies. In addition to having the proper gear, there are many health and safety considerations. Any time you go into the field, you are going into an uncontrolled and potentially hostile environment, and you need to take some basic steps to protect yourself and your collecting companions.

Sunscreen is one of the most effective and easy-to-use safety products, but many collectors still ignore its benefits. However, you need to put it on right away after you get to the site, or even better, before you leave the house. Many sites, especially the floors of open pit mines, act like giant solar reflectors, and the sun can be very intense. I also highly recommend a good pair of dark **sunglasses.** I cannot spend any time at all in an area of light-colored rocks if I do not have my sunglasses. Likewise, if you are not wearing a hard hat, wear a baseball cap or other hat for protection from the sun.

Although sun is often an issue, rain is often a bigger issue. I highly recommend having an **umbrella** handy. I know it sounds ridiculous, but I have gone on many extended hikes in the woods in driving rain with an umbrella, and this helped a great deal. An umbrella can make a big difference in the quality of your trip, especially when you are with friends or kids that may not enjoy a soaking rainstorm.

Speaking of rain, **lightning** can also be a significant concern. Many of the sites in this book are along the beaches of the Atlantic, Chesapeake Bay, and the Potomac River, and these areas are routinely exposed to strong thunderstorms and lightning. An umbrella will not help you if there is lightning. The best defense is to monitor the local forecast and get to a safe place long before the lightning arrives. Assuming you have a smartphone, you should be able to view radar maps that can warn you in advance of approaching storms. Your car will protect you from lightning, but bear in mind that most thunderstorms also come with strong winds, and you have to stay away from trees that can blow down on your vehicle. Every year people in the region are killed by both lightning strikes and falling trees.

Poison ivy can be a serious problem in the mid-Atlantic region. Poison ivy usually grows on the borders of outcrops and rocks, and this is another good reason to wear gloves. In fact, if your gloves have had extensive contact with the poison ivy, you may just have to throw them away.

While I always enjoy collecting in shorts and short-sleeve shirts, many sites are hidden among briars and other plants that can make your experience miserable if your legs and arms are exposed. I recommend always having a pair of **long pants** and a **light jacket** available if you need it, and you can also anticipate that these clothes will soon get ripped to shreds by thorns, broken branches, and sharp rocks. Long pants and sleeves can also help protect you from the sun and insects as well as flying rock chips from hammering.

Ticks are a major concern in the northeastern United States. During tick season, which seems to vary from place to place, I often find that I have been exposed to ticks as I am driving away from the site and see several crawling on my arms and legs just as I am entering traffic. Lyme disease is a serious issue, and you have to be on your guard at all times. The larger wood ticks, while not aesthetically pleasing, are typically not carriers of Lyme disease, while the much smaller deer ticks are known carriers. Rocky Mountain spotted fever, another serious tick-borne illness, is often carried by dog ticks, which are much larger than deer ticks. If you find a tick embedded in you, and it has been there for more than twenty-four hours, you may be at risk. Keep an eye on the bite mark, and contact your physician if it gets worse over the next few days.

To remove a tick, grasp the skin around the insertion of the tick with a pair of fine-point tweezers and pull straight outward, but be careful not to squeeze the tick body, as it may inject germs into the skin. Using an insect repellant that contains DEET is a good defense, as is light-colored clothing so you can quickly spot and remove the ticks. But even with insect repellent, you can still get bit. I received a Lyme tick bite in 2013 and had a bright red circle on my shoulder almost immediately. My doctor put me on antibiotics and apparently this took care of it, but I never even saw the tick.

Insect repellant with DEET is also good to keep away the **mosquitoes,** which may be present at any sites near standing water. Mosquitoes can also come out in force a few days after heavy rains. I have been on many trips that had nearly been ruined because I did not have ready access to insect repellant. Insect repellant wipes are also good to keep in your backpack if you are prone to forgetting repellant or if you do not want to carry around an entire bottle of repellant. West Nile virus, which is carried by mosquitoes, is also a serious threat. Spraying by state authorities has often dramatically reduced the numbers of mosquitoes, but if you are in an area that has not been sprayed and the mosquitoes are out, you will be in for a miserable trip if you are not protected. In extreme cases a mosquito net might be appropriate, but I have not been in any parts of Delaware, Maryland, or the DC area where I felt a net would be necessary, and insect repellant has always seemed to be sufficient.

An **orange or yellow safety vest** is important for any site where you are collecting along a roadside or any site that may be exposed to traffic or heavy equipment. Roads will always be dangerous, and many of the sites in this guide are at roadcuts. Provided you park in a safe place and stay well off the road, you should not have a problem, and the safety vest may alert cars to your presence. Curious onlookers may also assume that you are a highway worker or other employee just out doing their job and not question why you are so intently studying a roadcut.

Dehydration and **hunger** can make you and your companions miserable. Make sure that you and your collecting companions bring enough bottled water, and if you will be out all day, bring something to eat. Nearly all of the sites in this guidebook are near cities and places where you can get lunch, and most trips are half-day trips, so hunger is generally not a problem. Water, on the other hand, can be a problem. I generally have at least one half-liter of bottled water in my backpack and often take two half-liters of bottled water, and make sure that my collecting companions also have bottled water. I know this sounds obvious, but it is not a good situation to be miles from the car and not have water for a thirsty person that you have introduced to rockhounding. Never, ever drink water from streams, no matter how remote or how good it looks, unless you are equipped with a proper filter.

Getting to the site safely is important. The parking areas for the sites in this book can all be easily reached with a two-wheel-drive vehicle. It seems obvious, but if you are driving to a site, be sure your vehicle will get you there and that you have **plenty of gas.** I always try to keep my tank topped off. Gas stations are relatively easy to find, but I do not like it when my tank gets low. If you are taking more than one vehicle, make certain that there will be enough parking for two cars. Many drives are also very long, so if you get tired, be sure to pull over at a secure rest area and take a break.

While many collecting sites are in somewhat rural areas, some of the sites in this book are in urban settings. You should always be aware of your surroundings, make sure your vehicle is parked in a secure place, keep your vehicle GPS hidden, not leave valuables visible in your car, and be alert for suspicious characters. Generally if you have a bad feeling about where you parked your car, you will find that feeling has been justified when you return.

Underground mines are generally a nonissue in Delaware, Maryland, and DC, as most of the unstable mines collapsed or were closed many decades ago, and many of the open mines now have bat gates or other structures that keep people out. However, it is still possible to come across open portals and shafts, especially in some of the coal districts of western Maryland. The best policy is to stay outside of any underground workings.

Finally, you have to be careful when dealing with sites on **private property.** Always ask permission when you can, and be prepared to get yelled at or have other unpleasant experiences with landowners. Many of my most unpleasant experiences have involved dealing with their large and quite vicious dogs. Nearly all the landowners I have talked with have been good about giving permission, but every now and then I come across unfriendly owners. This challenge comes with the hobby, so if you are going to look for rocks on private lands and ask their owners for access, you have to be ready to deal with difficult people.

IMPORTANT ONLINE TOOLS

Many mineral and fossil localities have recently disappeared into developments, yet in that same time frame it's become much easier to find new sites. Google, Yahoo, Google Earth, and Google Maps all can be accessed to identify sites and explore potential localities.

I have found Google Maps to be especially helpful, but as of 2014 I am still using classic Google Maps instead of the latest version, as I have found the latest iteration of their maps to be far too clunky and slow. I always check the site using both the map and the satellite views. The map views are great, as they can show the street names and boundaries of public property, such as local and state parks. The satellite views are extremely useful, as you can zoom in and clearly see key items such as open pits, mine dumps, and signs of disturbance that may indicate historic or recent soil excavation and movement. Many sites, especially when minerals or fossils cover a broad area, are often exposed unexpectedly, and the satellite views in Google Maps can be a quick check to see recent exposures. Unfortunately these are not real-time photographs, and they are generally at least a year or two old. However, they are still much better than many maps and aerial photographs that may be decades old.

I have purposely left website addresses and phone numbers out of this guide, as web addresses expire, phone numbers change, and it is usually easy to find a web address via a search engine. Running an Internet search on a locality often brings up new and important updates, especially if a site has changed land status.

Likewise, all of the references cited in this book refer to the actual publication and do not provide a web address for access, unless the only available reference is the website itself. If you type in the citations or key parts of them, you can often access them online. If not, you can generally get them through your state library. I have found that a few publications are now only available on microfiche, but your librarian can often arrange for a copy to be e-mailed to you.

GEOLOGY

The person that turns over the most rocks wins the game.

—Peter Lynch

Some basic understanding of the geology of Delaware, Maryland, and Washington, DC, will help you understand why you encounter certain rocks, minerals, and fossils in various parts of the region. The area lies within five main geologic provinces, and this guidebook describes the geology of these provinces as opposed to just the geology of individual states. These are the Atlantic Coastal Plain, Piedmont, Blue Ridge, Ridge and Valley, and Appalachian Plateau.

ATLANTIC COASTAL PLAIN

The Atlantic Coastal Plain Province makes up all but the northern end of Delaware and much of southern and eastern Maryland. The province consists of a wedge of unconsolidated sediments that overlaps the rocks of the eastern Piedmont along an irregular line of contact known as the Fall Zone or Fall Line.

The Fall Line is an important geologic feature that has had a huge impact on the history of the region. In the early days of what later became the United States, water was the principal route of transport. Once you left the ocean and headed to the interior, the best way to move goods and people was up and down the river. Many of our mightiest rivers became key trading routes. Major rivers like the Mississippi, the Ohio, and the Hudson could be navigated along much of their route. However, boat traffic up the Susquehanna and Potomac was quickly stopped by the hard rocks of the Piedmont that were exposed beneath the Coastal Plain sediments.

Many rapids and waterfalls occurred at the Fall Line, which, as its name implies, provides the sudden drop for the water to fall. These stops became natural places for settlements, and the associated waterfalls also had the benefit of providing energy for mills. Many locks would ultimately be built to circumvent the falls, but of course this took a lot more time and energy, and in the meantime settlements could be established. The Fall Line in Delaware and Maryland traces a rough path from Wilmington to Baltimore and then to the

Great Falls of the Potomac. North of this line you will encounter the rocks of the Piedmont and the other geologic provinces, and south of this line you will find the Coastal Plain sediments.

As you go eastward from the Fall Line, the Atlantic Coastal Plain sediments get thicker, and are more than 8,000 feet thick along the Atlantic coast of Maryland. These sediments continue to thicken as they extend to the edge of the continental shelf, which extends eastward for another 75 miles. The sediments reach a maximum thickness of about 40,000 feet at the end of the continental shelf.

The sediments of the Atlantic Coastal Plain dip eastward at a very low angle, and range from Triassic to Quaternary. As you head southeast, the sediments become progressively younger. Quaternary sand and gravel covers many of the older formations throughout much of the Atlantic Coastal Plain, and you will only be able to see the older sediments in sections that have been cut either by streams, roads, or in some cases, canals.

Rockhounding in the Atlantic Coastal Plain is principally for fossils, but there are also some interesting mineral occurrences of vivianite, iron ores, and beach quartz. Sea glass, also known as beach glass, can also be found on many of the beaches on Chesapeake and Delaware Bay next to old tourist cities and early settlements. Sea glass gets polished and rounded much like quartz pebbles and can be very beautiful, especially when you find beach-polished glass of the rarer colors like blue, purple, and red. The author of *Pure Sea Glass*, Richard LaMotte, actually did much of his sea glass collecting on Chesapeake Bay. The reworking of very old rocks and relatively new glass has produced many very interesting beaches to visit on the Delaware, Maryland, and DC-area shorelines.

PIEDMONT

The Piedmont Province forms the northern end of Delaware, much of northeastern and central Maryland, and the northern sections of the Washington, DC, area. The Piedmont is composed of hard, crystalline igneous and metamorphic rocks and extends from the western edge of the Atlantic Coastal Plain to the long, northeast–southwest mountain range formed by Catoctin Mountain, which also represents the eastern border of the Blue Ridge Province. The rocks in the eastern part of the Piedmont are mainly schist, gneiss, and gabbro, as well as other highly metamorphosed rocks. The rocks in the western part of the Piedmont include phyllite, slate, marble, and moderately to slightly metamorphosed volcanic rocks.

The Piedmont rocks, due their age and complex metamorphic history, can be very difficult for geologists to map and understand. Unraveling the geologic history of the Piedmont is also complicated by the fact that the Piedmont rocks lie within some of the most heavily developed areas of the northeastern United States. Sometimes even the smallest outcrop can be an important clue to identifying the minerals and the structure of the underlying bedrock.

The Piedmont has many of the key mineral localities in this book. Iron, chromite, copper, and even gold were extracted from rocks of the Piedmont. Many of these former mines are now good collecting sites, and rockhounds can also find some interesting minerals in pegmatites that have intruded the metamorphic and igneous rocks of the Piedmont.

BLUE RIDGE

The Blue Ridge Province is the smallest of the geologic provinces, and is a relatively narrow band of lower Cambrian and Precambrian rocks that lie between the Piedmont and Ridge and Valley Province. The eastern boundary of the Blue Ridge is Catoctin Mountain and the western boundary is South Mountain, and it extends through northern Maryland and the area west of Washington, DC. Catoctin Mountain and South Mountain are formed by the limbs of a large anticline, and the ranges consist of hard, weather-resistant Lower Cambrian quartzite. The core of the anticline is principally Precambrian gneiss and volcanic rocks, and these are less resistant to erosion than the quartzite and form a broad valley.

Mineral deposits in the Blue Ridge Province are generally limited to iron ores and construction aggregates. Much of the area is either forested or developed, and it is a difficult area in which to find rock exposures. However, where the rocks are exposed, rockhounds will typically find deposits of goethite, slag, and some interesting late Precambrian–early Paleozoic rocks such as metabasalts and metarhyolite in the Blue Ridge.

RIDGE AND VALLEY

The Ridge and Valley Province consists of folded sediments that range in age from Lower Ordovician to Mississippian. These rocks form a series of ridges and valleys that trend northeast–southwest. The ridges are formed by the more resistant sandstones and conglomerates, while the valleys are formed in the less resistant carbonates and shales. Many of the railroads in the area parallel the resistant ridges and in some cases have some very sharp bends where they turn along the topography to get to the next ridge.

Rockhounding in the Ridge and Valley is generally limited to fossils, but there are some small deposits of iron and barite that can be good collecting sites if you are able to find and access them. The fossils are generally going to be found in the carbonates and shales, while the sandstones and conglomerates are generally not the types of rocks that will contain fossils. There are some sandy limestones and fine-grained clastic rocks that do have fossils, but these tend to be more the exception than the rule.

APPALACHIAN PLATEAU

The Appalachian Plateau Province is a broad uplift that has been dissected by streams and valleys. The bedrock of this region consists principally of shale, siltstone, and sandstone that are either horizontal or slightly folded. Several coal seams are found in the rock sequences as well, and many of these have been exploited by both underground and strip mines.

Rockhounding in this province is generally limited to fossils. I found that many of the fossils sites were on private land, and I did not get to thoroughly search this area to find accessible roadcuts or other sites with good minerals or fossils. Unless you are a local, this part of Maryland is relatively remote, and I was not able to locate any fossil sites in the Appalachian Plateau Province for this book.

NATURAL RESOURCES

> *Fifty years ago Geology was in its infancy; there were but few who cultivated it as a Science . . . If an unfortunate lover of nature was seen hammering in a stone quarry, he was generally supposed to be slightly demented.*
>
> —Peter Bellinger Brodie, 1858

Delaware, Maryland, and the Washington, DC, area were among the first areas of the United States to be mined for iron, copper, and gold, and the building materials industry supplied stone for many important buildings in Washington, Baltimore, and other cities in the region. When collecting minerals and fossils, it is often important to understand the underlying reasons for the location of mines and quarries. This will often help you identify the types of rocks you will encounter and give you some history lessons at the same time.

IRON

Like many of the original states, iron was the first metal to be mined in the Delaware and Maryland region. Iron mining in Delaware and Maryland dates back to the early 1700s. Bog iron was relatively easy to find in swampy areas of the Atlantic Coastal Plain in Delaware and Maryland , and many iron furnaces were built. The limiting factor for many mines was often the availability of charcoal for fuel and carbonate material for flux. The carbonate flux would reduce the melting temperature of the slag and remove many of the impurities from the iron. Along the coastal areas, some furnaces used oyster shells instead of limestone for flux, as suitable deposits of carbonate rock were often not available.

The bog iron ores were generally very poor quality, however, and while they contained iron, they were mainly composed of sediments and were ultimately too difficult to process into quality iron products. Larger, richer deposits of goethite and limonite were soon discovered in the mountains of the Piedmont in both states, as well as the Blue Ridge Province in Maryland. These areas also had abundant forests to produce charcoal and much larger deposits of limestone to make flux. Iron production continued up to the early twentieth century at some of these mines.

The goethite and limonite ores, while a slight improvement over the bog iron ores, soon found that they could not compete with the richer iron ores that were later discovered in some of the magnetite and hematite mines in Pennsylvania and New York. The discovery of these richer iron deposits quickly made the Delaware and Maryland mines uneconomical, and the vast iron mines that were then developed in the Lake Superior region ultimately doomed the Pennsylvania and New York mines as well. Today the remnants of iron mines in Delaware and Maryland can be seen at some of the former quarries that exploited the goethite and limonite, and glassy slag from many of their furnaces is also relatively easy to find near the old furnaces and along the streams near the furnaces.

COPPER

Copper was not mined in Delaware, but was mined from the colonial period until the mid-nineteenth century in Maryland. The Maryland copper mines were tiny compared to the large copper mines in Michigan and the American Southwest, but they were an important local source of copper when they were mined. The most productive copper mining areas were in Frederick County and Carroll County, and another small copper mine was located in the Bare Hills district in Baltimore County.

The former copper mines in Frederick County are all on private land and cannot be accessed without permission, but some of the former mines in Carroll County, such as the Mineral Hill mine, can be accessed by collectors. The former copper mining area around the Bare Hills has very limited access, and the mines and dumps have been obliterated by the construction of a large apartment complex and nearby roads.

GOLD

Gold was discovered in Maryland around 1849 near Brookville, which is north of Washington, DC, and within the Piedmont Province. This was also at about the same time as the greatest gold rush in history in California, and the Maryland gold mines were just not big enough to attract the same amount of attention. During the Civil War, Union soldiers camped near the Great Falls of the Potomac found gold at what became the Maryland Mine, which became the largest of the area gold mines. Several other lode and placer mines were developed in the region, but none remain in operation today. Gold is also reported to occur as placer deposits in Harford and Cecil Counties.

Being just north of Washington, DC, the area of Montgomery County with the gold mines is heavily developed. If you are not on private land, you are likely on federal government land, and much of this is within Great Falls National Park near the Potomac. Most of the former gold mines and their associated drainages are not accessible for recreational collecting, and the Maryland Mine is fenced and you are not even allowed to look through the dumps.

Many people still find drainages to access and attempt to pan for gold in Maryland. In addition to Montgomery County, panners also look for gold in the Piedmont drainages of Harford and Cecil Counties. Gold panning is a lot of hard work, and in my experience the returns have been minimal. You have to remember that many of these gravels, if they had gold, were repeatedly worked and worked until virtually all the placer gold was removed. In the meantime, the streambeds were further eroded and replaced with silt and lighter sediments that further covered any remaining gold. The old prospectors did not miss much, and it is very hard to find a placer that has not been highly worked over. Still, gold has that allure, and at any given time there is probably someone still trying their luck panning for gold in Maryland.

COAL

Coal has been mined in Maryland since the early nineteenth century. Coal deposits occur in the western end of Maryland in Garrett, Allegany, and Washington Counties. Coal production peaked in 1907, and more than 450 mines operated in Maryland at that time. As of 2014, only about sixty-five coal mines remain active in Maryland, and the state ranked nineteenth among coal-producing states. Its total coal production was only 0.2 percent of all the coal mined in the United States.

Coal mines often produce voluminous mine dumps, and fossil plants can often be found in the dumps and on the hillsides of former and active mines. Minerals such as barite, sphalerite, siderite, and calcite can sometimes be found in coal mines as well. Unfortunately many of these sites are private, and the active mines are inaccessible without special permission.

CONSTRUCTION AGGREGATES, CEMENT, AND BUILDING STONE

Delaware and Maryland geology—combined with their long history, major cities, and constant road and residential development—has made the aggregates, cement, and building stone industries by far the most profitable of all natural resources in the region. The Atlantic Coastal Plain deposits have significant amounts of sand and gravel, while the Piedmont has several major quarries that produce very hard stone for aggregates. The Piedmont quarries offer significant variety, as their various materials include granitic gneiss, serpentine, and marble. However, with transportation as a limiting factor, most of the rocks used by the quarries remain in their local market. Many additional quarries in the Blue Ridge, Ridge and Valley, and Appalachian Plateau Provinces also supply stone. Cement manufacturing is mainly limited to plants in Frederick, Carroll, and Washington Counties.

The building stone industry, which is also known as the dimension stone industry, was significant in the nineteenth century and first half of the twentieth century. Regional quarries, mainly in the Piedmont Province of Maryland, produced and exported granite, marble, quartzite, sandstone, and slate. Many of these stones took on the names of their location, such as Baltimore gneiss, Port Deposit "granite" (which is actually a gneiss), and Cockeysville marble. However, new technologies and less demand have greatly diminished the importance of large building and dimension stones.

Many of the former quarries offer excellent opportunities to see rocks but are often on federal or state land, and while you can get access, you may not be allowed to collect rocks. Private land requires permission for access, and active quarries, while they are among the best places to collect minerals, are increasingly restricting access.

HOW TO USE THIS GUIDE

Get away to the fields. Seek to decipher the geological records for yourself, and look with your own eyes into the long series of ages whose annals lie inscribed among the rocks. If you can secure the co-operation of a few companions, so the much the better . . . But whether singly or in company, use your eyes and your hammer, and even though in the end you should never become a geologist, you will in the meantime gain health and vigour, and a clearness of observation, that will stand you in good stead through life.

—Sir Archibald Geikie, 1858

The sites are listed by their location in the physiographic provinces, and are generally numbered westward from Delaware to northern and then southern Maryland, and then from western Maryland to the area around Washington, DC. Site names are often based on the nearest town, but in some cases I have used a local geographic feature for the locality name, especially if this will help collectors with locating the site. Maps with the localities have also been provided to help you plan site visits.

Each site entry gives **GPS coordinates** for parking, and if necessary, coordinates for the site itself, should you need to hike there. The coordinates are the latitude and longitude and are provided in the degrees, minutes, and seconds format, in the World Geodetic System (WGS 84) datum. The coordinates are rounded to the nearest second. Enter the coordinates in your GPS device, and they will take your vehicle on a route to the site. However, be aware that some GPS systems will take you on back roads and trails, and these may not be the best route to the site. In some cases, especially in rural areas, they may take you on roads and trails that may not even be made for motor vehicles.

Make sure that you understand how to use your GPS, especially when using coordinates. For some reason, some users know how to enter a street address but do not know how to enter a latitude and longitude. Sometimes latitude and longitude are given in decimal degrees or in degrees decimal minutes, and you have to understand what you are entering. You may have to do a conversion to the correct format, but this is very simple, provided you understand basic algebra. Often the GPS will give you a preview of where you are going after you enter the coordinates, and you should check this to see if it looks correct. If it is taking you out to sea, into a big field, or into a bunch of buildings in Wilmington, Baltimore, or Washington, DC, you may have entered the coordinates incorrectly. It is very easy to enter the coordinates incorrectly, but fortunately this is easy to fix, provided you catch it before you go too far.

The **finding the site** section can be a good partner to your GPS as you plan your trip. In this section, a route to each site is given from a major highway or, occasionally, from a nearby city. Depending on where you have started, the site may be between you and that starting point, so it is a good idea to supplement the GPS and these directions with a good state highway map.

I have personally visited every site in this book. The GPS coordinates were checked against topographic maps and satellite photos, and they are correct. In addition, the road directions in the "finding the site" entries were verified. The directions were originally obtained by the way that I went to the site, and then verified using detailed mileages and directions from Google Maps.

I often found that the location information provided in other field guides or geologic publications was either incorrect, too vague, or purposely left out to keep collectors away. I have also included GPS coordinates for both the parking area and the site itself for the locations that merit both. In many cases the parking area is the same as the site, whereas in some cases you have to first park and then hike a significant distance to the site. I sometimes had to visit a site multiple times before I found the right location, and even then I was sometimes unsure if I had made it to the right spot. You may use this guide and in some cases find that the spot I recommended was not as good as an adjacent location, despite my efforts to find the best spot.

The site descriptions can be used to quickly provide information about a site so you will know what to expect during your visit. The **site type** refers to the type of occurrence, and this generally is a physical description of the site, which may be a streambed, roadcut, former quarry, or outcrop. The **land status** is based on the best available information and should let you know if you will be able to access the site without special permission or if you need to secure approval from a site owner for access. In many cases the official status of a parcel is not known, and these sites generally have access but no guarantee that they are actually open to visitors.

The **material** refers to the type of minerals, rocks, or fossils that a visitor would likely find of most interest. If they are listed, I can assure you that they are present at the site, but it still may take some effort to find them. In some cases if a mineral or fossil is reported to be present at a site but I did not find it, I have listed it as "reported" if the geologic conditions are appropriate for that mineral or fossil to be present. Just because I did not find it does not mean it is not there.

The **host rock** is the rock in which the material is found, and I have generally named the geologic formation or type of rock that best describes the enclosing rocks as the host rock. It is important to understand what rocks host your materials of interest, as you can use this knowledge to find similar sites.

The **difficulty** level is a guide to the likelihood of finding or observing the materials referenced in the site description. Some sites are loaded with material and you can step onto the site and find as much as you could possibly desire. Other sites take hours and hours of effort to find a single specimen, and even your most diligent efforts are not a guarantee that you will find or observe anything. If a site is marked as difficult, be aware that it may not be a good site for impatient collectors.

The **family-friendly** rating is very subjective and depends entirely upon your family. If the description says yes without any qualifiers, you will generally find this to be a site where you can take small children and family members that can handle moderate walking and want to look at rocks. These sites also tend to be among the easier sites to find rocks. If the description says no, generally this is because the minerals or fossils are very hard to find, or because site access is very limited or difficult.

The **tools needed** field will let you know what kind of collecting tools you should bring to a site. In most cases a rock hammer and gloves are all that is needed, but for some sites you may be best served with a chisel, flat-bladed screwdriver, large sledgehammer, or shovel. At some sites, such as in beach gravels that are screened, you do not need a hammer. I do not list standard safety equipment like boots, safety glasses, or hard hats here, as the emphasis is on tools. Unfortunately some sites do not allow collecting, so in these cases this field is simply "none." I usually bring my rock hammer, gloves, and day pack to virtually all sites, or at least keep them in reserve in the car if needed.

I have also included a section on **special concerns** so you know why this may not be a good site for everyone, especially if you are bringing small children, impatient collectors, or friends or family that may not appreciate the more adventurous aspects of rockhounding. This does not mean you should not take your family, but be prepared to deal with the issues mentioned in the site description.

If collecting at a site is not allowed, it is mentioned in the special concerns section. As mentioned previously, do not assume that this guide gives you permission to collect or access the property. In general, all public sites in this guide can be accessed and you can look at the rocks, but many parks and government sites do not allow collecting or disturbing rocks. If the site is private, do not enter posted areas without obtaining permission, and be aware that some private ground is not often clearly posted against trespassing. In many areas ownership and the rules regarding rock collecting are not clear, so if collecting regulations are unclear at any of these sites, leave your hammer in the car and simply enjoy looking at the rocks.

Map Legend

Symbol	Feature	Symbol	Feature
95	Interstate Highway		Airport
40	US Highway		National Capital
97	State Highway		State Capital
13	County/Local Road		Point of Interest
	Railroad	1	Rockhounding Site
	State Line		Town
	County Line		Cemetery
	Body of Water		Military Base
	River/Creek		National Wildlife Refuge
	Intermittent Stream		State Park/State Forest
	Intracoastal Waterway		Wildlife Management Area
	Ferry		

DELAWARE

White Clay Creek, northwestern Delaware (Site 5). Delaware rocks range from Late Precambrian granitic and metamorphic rocks to recent coastal sediments, and offer a wide range of opportunities for rockhounds.

Delaware

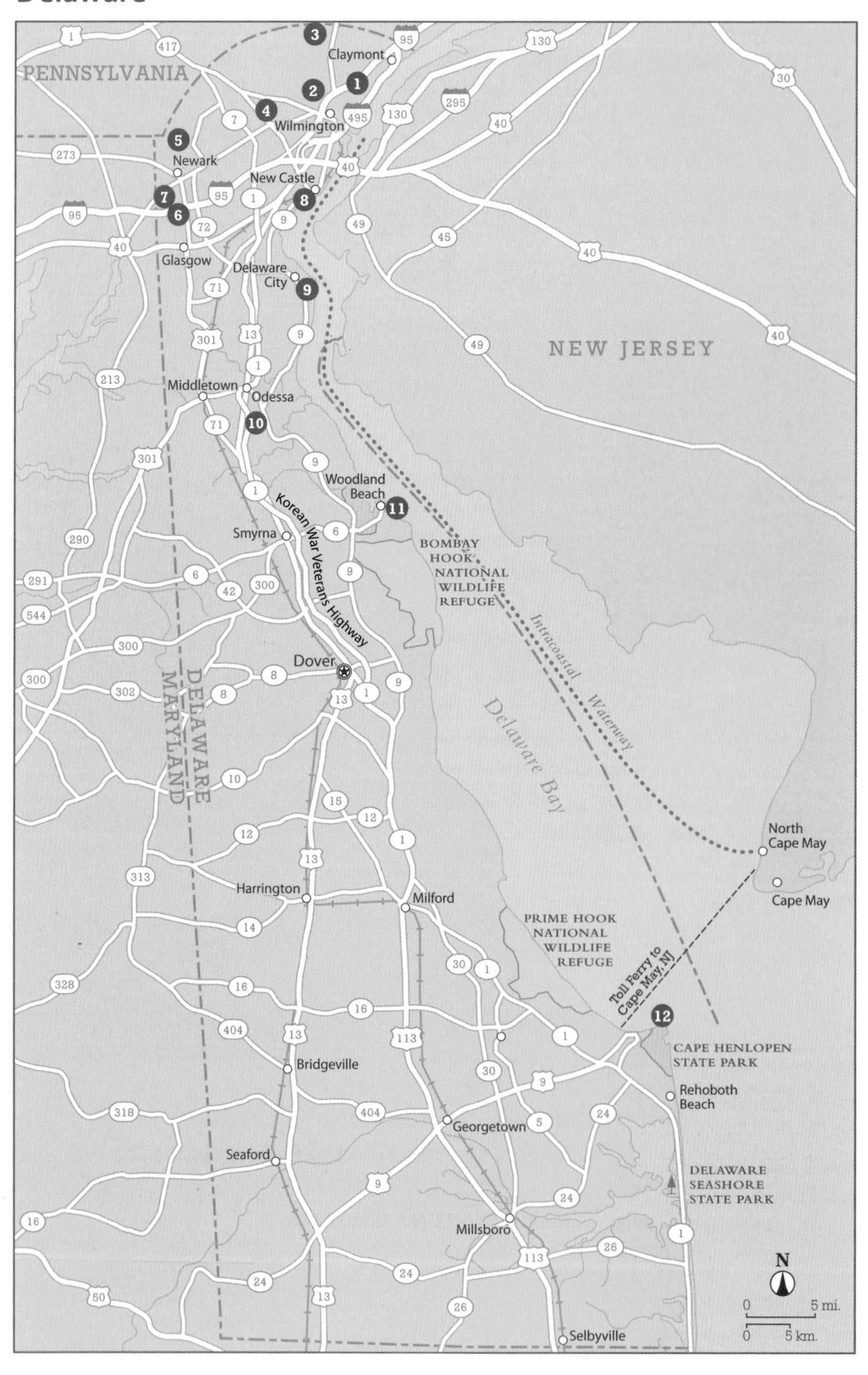

PENNSYLVANIA
NEW JERSEY
DELAWARE
MARYLAND
Claymont
Wilmington
Newark
New Castle
Glasgow
Delaware City
Middletown
Odessa
Woodland Beach
Smyrna
Korean War Veterans Highway
Dover
Harrington
Milford
Bridgeville
Georgetown
Seaford
Millsboro
Selbyville
Rehoboth Beach
North Cape May
Cape May
BOMBAY HOOK NATIONAL WILDLIFE REFUGE
Intracoastal Waterway
Delaware Bay
PRIME HOOK NATIONAL WILDLIFE REFUGE
Toll Ferry to Cape May, NJ
CAPE HENLOPEN STATE PARK
DELAWARE SEASHORE STATE PARK
N
0 5 mi.
0 5 km.

1. Wilmington Bringhurst Gabbro

Shellpot Creek is full of boulders of Bringhurst gabbro, and is easy to reach from the parking area.

County: New Castle
Site type: Boulders in stream
Land status: Bringhurst Woods Park
Material: Pyroxene phenocrysts
Host rock: Bringhurst gabbro
Difficulty: Easy
Family-friendly: Yes
Tools needed: None
Special concerns: Park property; no hammering of rocks allowed
Special attractions: Wilmington state parks, including the Brandywine Zoo
GPS parking: 39°46'35"N / 75°30'39"W
GPS gabbro in Shellpot Creek: 39°46'33"N / 75°30'38"W
Topographic quadrangle: Wilmington North, DE–PA

Finding the site: From I-95 north, take exit 9 to DE 3/Marsh Road. Turn right (south) and proceed about 0.3 mile, then turn right onto Carr Road. Go about 0.2 mile, and the parking area will be on your left (south). From I-95 south, take exit 9 as well, but turn left (south) onto DE 3, turn right onto Carr Road, and park in the parking area to the left (south). From the parking area, walk south to Shellpot Creek to the gabbroic boulders.

Rockhounding

This is an excellent stop to see coarse-grained gabbroic boulders with large orthopyroxene crystals. The Bringhurst gabbro is early Paleozoic in age, and is relatively undeformed when compared to the older igneous and metamorphic rocks in the region. The igneous structures are relatively well preserved in the gabbro. The pyroxene phenocrysts tend to be slightly more resistant to weathering than the plagioclase feldspar matrix, which results in rock surfaces where the crystals protrude from the matrix and are easily seen.

I stopped at this locality in April on a late afternoon weekday, and the park was nearly deserted. Shellpot Creek and the rocks are just south of the parking area, and it was very easy to walk down to the creek, which was full of boulders, and see the coarse-grained gabbroic rocks. From a slight distance the rocks appear dark green to black, but when you get close you can see that the aggregates of black minerals protrude from the dark gray groundmass. The minerals are best exposed on surfaces that have been subject to weathering. Slightly farther upstream from the parking area is a power line; this area has been cleared and the rocks are very well exposed here. Unfortunately, as this is a park, hammering the rocks and collecting is not allowed, but the rocks are still so unusual that the site is well worth a visit.

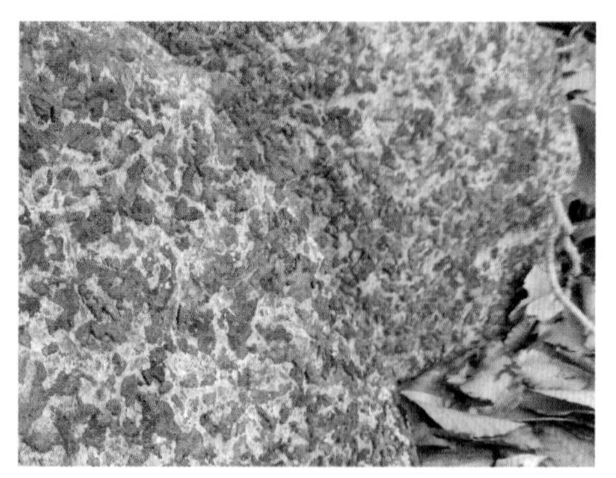
The Bringhurst gabbro has coarse phenocrysts of pyroxene, and some are nearly 2 inches long.

References: Woodruff and Thompson, 1975; Ramsey, 2005

Sites 1–9

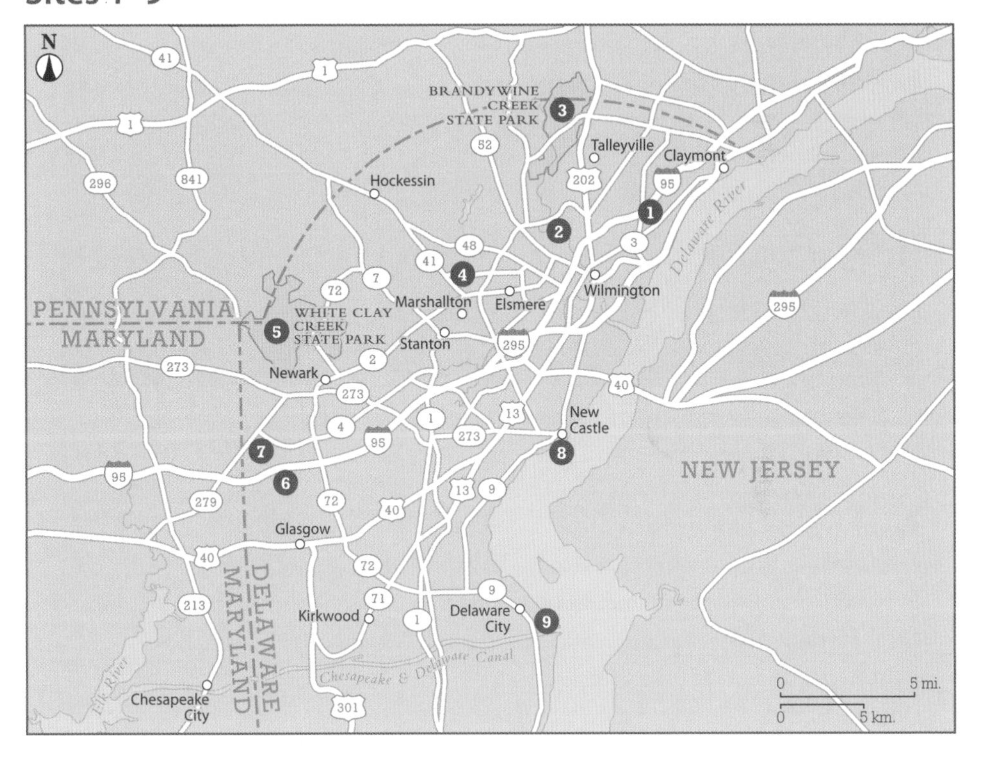

N
BRANDYWINE CREEK STATE PARK
Talleyville
Claymont
Hockessin
Delaware River
Marshallton
Elsmere
Wilmington
PENNSYLVANIA
MARYLAND
WHITE CLAY CREEK STATE PARK
Stanton
Newark
New Castle
NEW JERSEY
Glasgow
DELAWARE
MARYLAND
Kirkwood
Delaware City
Chesapeake & Delaware Canal
Elk River
Chesapeake City
0 5 mi.
0 5 km.

2. Wilmington Blue Gneiss

Brandywine Creek can be deep near this area of Wilmington blue gneiss.

See map page 29.
County: New Castle
Site type: Outcrops along Brandywine Creek
Land status: Alapocas Woods Park, a Delaware state park
Material: Brandywine blue gneiss
Host rock: Early Paleozoic gneiss of the Wilmington Group
Difficulty: Easy
Family-friendly: Yes
Tools needed: None; collecting not allowed
Special concerns: Trail to creek can be steep, water is deep next to rocks
Special attractions: Wilmington Blue Rocks baseball, fishing in Brandywine Creek
GPS parking: 39°46'25"N / 75°33'59"W
GPS site: 39°46'14"N / 75°34'07"W

Topographic quadrangle: Wilmington North, DE–PA

Finding the site: From I-95, take exit 8B for US 202 North/Concord Pike. Go about 0.8 mile, keep right at the fork, and follow the signs for DE 261 North/Foulk Road. Go about 0.1 mile, keep left, and follow the signs for DE 141 South. Turn left onto DE 141 South, go about 1.6 miles, and turn left (southeast) onto Alapocas Drive. Take the second left just past Old County Road. This second left later intersects with Old County Road and may or may not have a sign. Follow the signs from here to the Alapocas Park ball fields, park in the parking lot, and take the trail that is on the southern side of the parking lot and heads southwest to Brandywine Creek. This is the quickest route to the creek from the parking area.

Rockhounding

Brandywine blue gneiss underlies much of Wilmington and the nearby area. The gneiss is known as "Wilmington blue rock," and the local minor-league baseball team, the Wilmington Blue Rocks, took its name from this blue gneiss. Their mascot is named (guess what?) "Rocky." The blue gneiss is well

Wilmington blue gneiss boulders line the creek bank in this area, and the large logs give an indication of the high-water mark during flooding.

exposed along Brandywine Creek, where it has cut a deep gorge from south of Rockland to the Market Street Bridge.

The gneiss is early Paleozoic and metasedimentary, and consists of medium- to coarse-grained granulites and gneisses that are mainly plagioclase, quartz, pyroxene, hornblende, magnetite, and ilmenite. The color is not really "blue," but the overall appearance of the gneiss is generally a light to medium gray, and the contrast with the nearby woods and water gives the rock a light blue appearance. Similar gneisses mined by the quarry industry in other states are often referred to as "bluestone."

While the rocks are well exposed along Brandywine Creek, I found that getting to large exposures could be a challenge, as parking is often limited and many of the areas along the creek are either private land or otherwise developed. One of the best localities that I found was by parking near the ball fields for Alapocas Park and hiking southwest down the trail directly to the creek. Alapocas Park is part of the Delaware State Parks system, and all associated state park rules will apply. You have to be careful to take the right trail; otherwise, you may just find yourself on a long, albeit pleasant, hike through the woods east of the creek but without any exposures of the blue gneiss. The trail from the ball fields ends near a small dam, and the gneiss is well exposed near this area of the creek. It is best to come to this area during relatively low water, as it is obvious that much of the area gets flooded.

This is also a local hangout for partiers along the creek, so you will likely see some other visitors on late afternoons and weekends, especially on hot days. However, in all likelihood they will have absolutely no interest in looking at the blue gneiss with you.

Reference: Schenck et al., 2000

3. Woodlawn Quarry Mica and Feldspar

The main quarry is flooded and has steep sides that are covered with silvery mica.

See map page 29.
County: New Castle
Site type: Former small quarry and prospect pits
Land status: First State National Monument
Material: Mica (nearly entirely muscovite), feldspar
Host rock: Pegmatites
Difficulty: Easy
Family-friendly: Yes
Tools needed: None
Special concerns: National monument; no collecting allowed
Special attractions: Brandywine Creek State Park
GPS parking: 39°49'45"N / 75°34'12"W

GPS site: 39°49'53"N / 75°33'50"W
Topographic quadrangle: Wilmington North, DE–PA
Finding the site: From I-95 north, take exit 8 for US 202 North/Concord Pike towards West Chester. Continue about 1.1 miles and follow the signs for DE 141 South, then merge onto US 202 North/Concord Pike. Continue 3 miles and turn left onto Rocky Run Parkway. Continue about 0.3 mile and turn left onto Woodlawn Road. Go about 0.5 mile and turn right onto DE 92 East. Go about 0.2 mile and turn left onto Ramsey Road. The parking area is approximately 0.8 mile farther west on the right (north) side Ramsey Road. Park here and hike through the woods to the quarry. The quarry is located in the woods approximately 2,000 feet northeast of the parking area.

Rockhounding

The Woodlawn Quarry is a former feldspar quarry that operated from about 1850 to 1910. The feldspar was mined and transported to Philadelphia for manufacturing porcelain products, but closed after other feldspar sites became more economical to operate. In 1910 the area around the quarry, which includes woods and fields, was bought by William Bancroft as a wildflower preserve. For many years this was a key site for mineral clubs for collecting mica and feldspar, but in 2013 it became part of the First State National Monument. Collecting minerals is no longer allowed at this site. However, it is a classic locality that it still well worth visiting and it is easy to access.

The quarry is in a pegmatite in the Wissahickon Formation, which is Lower Paleozoic metasedimentary schist. I visited the site in April 2014. Although the Delaware Geological Survey has a description of the site and a map, I found it very difficult to find the quarry with just their directions. The parking area on the north side of Ramsey Road is obvious, but there are no signs indicating the location of the quarry. I asked a hiker who was walking her dog if she knew of the quarry, but she said she did not. Suddenly she said, "Oh, now I think I know what you are asking about. There are some pits in the woods with shiny paper-like rocks." She agreed to take me to the pits, which were in the woods approximately 2,000 feet northeast of the parking area.

There is one very large water-filled pit and several small prospect pits in the quarry area. Much of the ground is covered with leaves, but you can easily see pieces of feldspar and muscovite mica on the ground, especially if you brush away some of the leaves in the pit. The woman who showed me the

Mica books can be observed in the leaves of some of the nearby prospect pits.

pits soon went back to hiking with her dog, and I had the chance to explore the rest of the area on my own. No other visitors came to the quarry, and I suspect this is due to the lack of directions at the parking area. Although it is now part of a national monument, it is still an excellent site to visit to see classic Delaware pegmatite minerals.

Reference: Schenk et al., 2000

4. Brandywine Springs Park Sillimanite

Sillimanite can be found among the rocks in the streambed of Hyde Run.

See map page 29.

County: New Castle

Site type: Stream rocks

Land status: Brandywine Springs Park

Material: Sillimanite

Host rock: Wissahickon Formation

Difficulty: Moderate

Family-friendly: Yes

Tools needed: None

Special concerns: Streambed is parkland; no collecting allowed in the park

Special attractions: Remnants of Brandywine Springs Amusement Park

GPS parking: 39°44'45"N / 75°38'33"W

GPS stream with sillimanite: 39°44'38"N / 75°38'08"W

Topographic quadrangle: Newark East, DE

Finding the site: From I-95, take exit 5B for DE 141 North. Merge onto DE 141 North/US 202 North and continue about 2.6 miles. Take exit 6B towards DE 2/DE 41, then take DE 2 towards DE 41 North. Merge onto DE 2 West, go about 0.7 mile, and turn right (northwest) onto DE 41 North (Newport Gap Pike). Go about 1 mile and turn right (east) onto DE 34 East (Faulkland Road). Go 0.1 mile and turn right into the main parking lot for Brandywine Springs County Park. The sillimanite can be found in Hyde Run, which is a creek reached by a short hike to the south from the parking area.

Rockhounding

This is one of the best sites in Delaware to see loose pieces of sillimanite in a streambed. Sillimanite is the state mineral of Delaware, so I consider this to be a must for any rockhound that visits northern Delaware. Sillimanite is an aluminum silicate with the chemical formula Al_2SiO_5, and it is a polymorph with kyanite and andalusite. Polymorphs are minerals that share the same chemical formula but have different mineral structures. Kyanite, andalusite, and sillimanite form at different temperatures and pressures, and this is useful to determine the intensity of metamorphism of the rock.

Brandywine Springs County Park and the surrounding area are underlain by early Paleozoic Faulkland gneiss, which is a fine- to coarse-grained amphibolite with felsic zones. The rock is likely metavolcanic in origin, and sillimanite formed in the felsic zones during intense high pressure and high temperature metamorphism. The sillimanite eventually eroded out of the gneiss, and pieces of sillimanite can now be found in the creek in and adjacent to Brandywine Springs Park. Unfortunately, as a county park, collecting of the sillimanite is not allowed.

This creek is Hyde Run, which is a tributary of Red Clay Creek. During my visit to the site, I hiked along the trails and the creek, and eventually hiked out the eastern side of the park and checked the creek outside the park boundaries just east of a small railroad bridge. None of this area was posted against trespassing, and I had no problem walking along this section of the creek. The light was much better here to see the rocks, as much of the park area is covered by trees. I checked the loose rocks in the creek and was getting pretty discouraged, but then I found a piece that was white and composed of a mass of fibrous aggregates, which were tightly intertwined fibers of sillimanite. It was very fine-grained and I had to look closely to see the

This piece of sillimanite shows good elongated fibers and was found in the creek bed of Hyde Run east of Brandywine Springs Park.

individual fibers. I then focused on looking for white pieces that were slightly elongated and soon found numerous pieces of sillimanite. Some of the pieces were somewhat iron-stained and the rocks had to be broken apart to expose fresh surfaces of sillimanite, and the rock interiors were also often iron-stained.

After I looked in the area outside of the park, I hiked west along the creek within the park boundaries and found similar pieces. It takes some effort to find sillimanite in the creek, and you have to be very careful if you walk on the rocks in the creek, especially in the areas with the largest boulders. The creek is obviously best to visit when the water is low.

The area was the site of a popular amusement park from approximately 1890 to 1923. Foundations of the bridges and former structures can be seen along the crushed-stone trails along Hyde Run. Today it is a popular local county park, and there are several signs along the path describing the history of the former amusement park. Many of these signs have old photographs that can be matched with current features, but the area has changed so much that it is difficult to easily match the old photos with the current topography along Hyde Run. It is hard to imagine that that park valley was once covered with buildings, boardwalks, and throngs of people.

Reference: Schenk et al., 2000

5. White Clay Creek Orange Feldspar

White Clay Creek narrows near Tweed's Mill Bridge, and large banks with feldspar-rich rocks form along the streambed.

See map page 29.
County: New Castle
Site type: Loose rocks in stream
Land status: White Clay Creek State Park
Material: Orange feldspar
Host rock: Pegmatitic rocks from the Wissahickon Formation
Difficulty: Easy
Family-friendly: Yes
Tools needed: None
Special concerns: State park; no collecting allowed
Special attractions: Fishing and swimming in White Clay Creek
GPS parking: 39°42'56"N / 75°45'37"W

GPS creek bank: 39°42'55"N / 75°45'31"W
GPS reported pegmatite dam: 39°43'05"N / 75°45'37"W
Topographic quadrangle: Newark West, DE–MD–PA
Finding the site: From Newark, head west on E. Main Street, which is DE 273. Turn right (northwest) onto DE 896 and head northwest for 2.2 miles. Turn right (east) onto Wedgewood Road. Follow this about 1 mile to where Wedgewood Road ends. The parking area is just to your left. Park here, pay the state park fee, and walk to the bridge that crosses White Clay Creek. This is also known as Tweed's Mill Bridge, and it is on the Tri-Valley Trail. The creek banks north of the bridge are covered with gneissic rocks and orange feldspar.

Rockhounding

White Clay Creek is named for the white kaolinitic clays that formed from the weathering of feldspar. The creek flows from Pennsylvania into Delaware and cuts through the late Precambrian granitic and metamorphic rocks of the Piedmont Province. As this is a Delaware state park, no rock collecting is allowed, but the park often sponsors geologic field trips for school students. I have been to the park several times, and one of the issues I have found with looking at the rocks in White Clay Creek in Delaware is that many parts of the creek are in a broad alluvial plain, and the banks and streambeds in these areas generally have very small rocks and sandy zones. The location referenced here is where White Clay Creek narrows and the banks are steeper, and large areas with orange feldspar boulders and pegmatitic rocks can easily be seen in the creek bed.

This orange feldspar shows excellent cleavage and was found in the streambed.

Many of these feldspar-rich rocks are a distinct orange, and the feldspar exhibits excellent cleavage. It is easy to find rocks that are nearly all feldspar, and they are mixed with the gneissic rocks and other late Precambrian metamorphic and late Paleozoic sedimentary clasts. To find the feldspar-rich rocks and pegmatitic rocks, look for the rocks with an orange cast and angular features, which are from the crystalline patterns of the feldspar. Rounded rocks are generally fine-grained gneisses and other rocks that do not have many prominent minerals.

After my visit to this locality, I learned that a pegmatite "dam" is also reportedly present upstream. Unfortunately I did not get to visit this dam, but I was able to make out the approximate coordinates on Google Earth and on the topographic map. It is only about 1,200 feet upstream, and it should be easy to reach by walking up the trails on either side of White Clay Creek. It appears to be a fairly substantial structure, but of course it has likely taken a beating over the past century. This dam would probably be another good place to see coarse-grained feldspar-rich rocks and pegmatite minerals.

References: Faill, 1991; Schenk et al., 2000

6. Iron Hill Goethite and Limonite

Bands of goethite can be found in the large boulders of iron ore.

See map page 29.

County: New Castle
Site type: Former iron mine
Land status: Iron Hill County Park
Material: Goethite and limonite
Host rock: Silurian Iron Hill gabbro
Difficulty: Easy
Family-friendly: Yes
Tools needed: None
Special concerns: County park; no collecting allowed
Special attractions: Iron Hill Museum
GPS parking: 39°38'20"N / 75°45'22"W
GPS large boulder in mine: 39°38'27"N / 75°45'19"W
GPS parking Iron Hill Museum: 39°37'53"N / 75°45'30"W
Topographic quadrangle: Newark West, DE–MD–PA
Finding the site: From I-95 South, take exit 1A to merge onto DE 896 South. Go about 1.1 miles and turn right (west) onto Old Baltimore Pike. Go about 0.8 mile and turn right into the entrance for the park. Proceed about 0.5 mile to the

parking area. From here follow the trail that leads northeast. You will see a large water-filled pit. Continue north and look for a gigantic boulder. This boulder is in the Whittaker ore pit, which was apparently one of the key mining areas on Iron Hill.

Rockhounding

Iron mining started at Iron Hill in 1703, which makes this one of the oldest industries in the Newark area. Miners worked the iron deposits for limonite, but the smelting was expensive, as no economical sources of flux were available. The deposit had the misfortune to be located in a region that was relatively devoid of easily accessible carbonate rocks for flux, unlike many of the other iron-mining regions in the northeast United States. The operation went bankrupt in the 1720s, and iron mining at Iron Hill was limited until 1837 when the railroads reached Newark. Ores could finally be shipped by rail to the Perryville smelter in Maryland. After 1850 the demand for iron in the United States greatly increased due to the vast needs for iron and steel by the

This large boulder is a prominent feature of the floor of one of the larger mining pits at Iron Hill.

railroad industry. However, the mines at Iron Hill were soon exhausted, and mining was then started in 1875 in Chestnut Hill (Site 7), which is just north of Iron Hill and has roughly similar geology.

This site has a tremendous amount of goethite and limonite, but no collecting is allowed, except on field trips sponsored by the Iron Hill Museum. The iron mines are very easy to reach from the parking area, but you have to follow the correct trails through the woods. This is where the map from the Iron Hill Museum, which is described below, comes in handy. The mine pit nearest the parking area is full of water, but a second pit, known as the Whittaker ore pit, is just north of the flooded pit. This pit has a gigantic boulder of goethite and limonite, and several smaller, albeit still very large, boulders are throughout the pit area. The goethite and limonite form an interesting pattern on many of the rocks and in some cases can be described as a honeycomb.

This site was also my introduction to another hobby known as geocaching. Clues to find the geocache are posted online. The large boulder had a plastic container with a small notebook and pen, and visitors who found the cache were invited to write in the notebook and leave a small item in the plastic box. Several people had found the box and left notes. The cache was found in one of the large honeycomb-like voids in the boulder, which made this a near-perfect site for a geocache.

Before you go to the mine area, if your schedule permits and it is open, take a tour of the Iron Hill Museum. This is an outstanding little museum with excellent Delaware mineral and fossil displays, and I was especially impressed with their assemblage of Delaware fossils. As mentioned above, you can also get a map of Iron Hill Park at the museum. Although the trails are marked, a map is very useful when visiting Iron Hill.

Reference: Schenk et al., 2000

7. Chestnut Hill Boxwork Limonite

Many of the limonitic rocks on the dump exhibit an intricate boxwork structure.

See map page 29.
County: New Castle
Site type: Former iron mines
Land status: Chestnut Hill Iron Pit Preservation (CHIPP)
Material: Boxwork limonite
Host rock: Iron Hill gabbro
Difficulty: Easy
Family-friendly: Yes
Tools needed: None; collecting not allowed
Special concerns: Steep slopes on hillsides, ticks and mosquitoes
Special attractions: Iron Hill Museum
GPS parking: 39°39'13.8"N / 75°46'24"W
GPS northern mine dump: 39°39'13"N / 75°46'21"W

Topographic quadrangle: Newark West, DE–MD–PA

Finding the site: From I-95 South, take exit 1B to merge onto DE 896. Turn right toward W. Chestnut Hill Road. This is an unusual turn, as you have to go right, circle back around, and then proceed onto west on W. Chestnut Hill Road. Proceed 1.1 miles on W. Chestnut Hill Road, then turn right onto University Drive. Go 0.6 mile and turn left onto Miners Lane. Go approximately 0.2 mile and park on the right (north) side of the road just west of the large stormwater basin. The entrance to the preserve is past the stormwater basin on the south side of Miners Lane, just past the fourth house west of the basin. A small sign marking the trailhead can be seen from Miners Lane.

Rockhounding

Chestnut Hill was the site of iron mining from 1875 to 1910. Iron ore had previously been mined at Iron Hill, and the deposits at Chestnut Hill were developed after the ores at Iron Hill had been exhausted. Unfortunately for the mine operators, the ores were relatively low-grade compared to deposits

The northern mine dump is full of limonitic rocks, and the orange-red soil is indicative of the high iron content of the rocks.

being mined elsewhere at the time. The deposits could not be economically mined to make steel, which was in great demand at that time.

This is a very unusual locality, as it is now a preserve that is located in a residential neighborhood. Chestnut Hill Iron Pit Preservation (CHIPP) was organized in the early 1990s to protect the lands around the former iron mines, and CHIPP was able to save an 8.6-acre tract from further development. In 2006 a Boy Scout helped establish trails and access into the mined area through his Eagle Scout project. I have found that many Eagle Scouts have done similar projects to build trails and preserve old mining sites, and these projects are always a tremendous service to those who want to preserve access to old mining sites. This was an excellent project, and it is very easy to walk around the former mines, which are now nearly entirely covered by woods.

When I first looked for this site, I was not aware of the trails to the mine, and I actually walked around the stormwater basin east of the site to look for goethite and limonite. I found some interesting pieces along the edge of the basin, but the basin was full of geese and it was not a pleasant place to look for rocks. As I got in my car and started driving away, I saw the trails to the Chestnut Hill mines. Unfortunately a huge thunderstorm was coming, and I had to cut my visit short. I came back the following weekend after I visited the Iron Hill mine, and found that both of these areas can easily be visited in a single day.

The iron mines at Chestnut Hill exploited near-surface deposits of highly oxidized iron ores of the Iron Hill gabbro. The Iron Hill gabbro is Silurian and is deeply weathered on Chestnut Hill. The mine area has several very large dumps of limonitic rocks, which have an unusual "boxwork" structure. I have seen this before in limestones and other weathered limonitic iron ores, but never to the degree that is present at Chestnut Hill. Throughout the mine area there are also many large boulders of limonite, and much of the soil is orange-brown to reddish brown, which is consistent with the iron-rich bedrock. Unfortunately, as it is a preserve, collecting is not allowed.

References: Day, n.d.; Schenk et al., 2000

8. New Castle Battery Park Beach Sea Glass

Much of the glass at this beach is still relatively recent and best classified as shards.

See map page 29.
County: New Castle
Site type: Beach
Land status: Battery Park
Material: Sea glass
Host rock: Beach along Battery Park
Difficulty: Easy
Family-friendly: Yes
Tools needed: Plastic bag to collect glass
Special concerns: Abundant glass shards, litter, dirty water; parking may be an issue
Special attractions: Battery Park and Old New Castle

Battery Park beach is very rocky, which is good for polishing of sea glass.

GPS parking: 39°39'35"N / 75°33'50"W
GPS beach: 39°39'26"N / 75°33'58"W
Topographic quadrangle: Wilmington South, DE–NJ
Finding the site: From I-95, take exit 5A toward DE 141 South/US 202 South. Continue down the exit until you reach DE 141 South and turn right (southeast). Continue 2.6 miles and turn left onto Delaware Street. Continue about 0.9 mile to the town of New Castle and park where you can find a space. Parking may be an issue during weekends or events, and you may have to park farther away and have a longer walk to the beach. Battery Park is along the shoreline.

Rockhounding

Battery Park is an old park established along the Delaware River shoreline at New Castle. Like many parks with similar names, such as Battery Park in Manhattan, it got its name from the artillery batteries that were stationed here long ago. This is one of the oldest settled areas in the United States, dating back to the mid-1600s. As such there is the potential for lots of glass and associated ceramics to have been dumped off the shoreline, which later washes up on the beach.

I had the opportunity to visit this park as the tide was receding. While this is a reported location for old sea glass, it also has an abundance of modern glass. Broken glass is abundant on the beach, and much of it is best described as glass shards as opposed to sea glass. I found a piece of broken blue glass and some frosted white, green, and brown glass, along with some ceramic pieces. I was surprised at the number of kids walking on the beach in bare feet. Due to its location on the northern end of Delaware Bay, the glass may not get the reworking that many other beaches get from wave action, but it does have the potential for older glass, and the abundance of rocks and pebbles certainly provides a good grinding medium to polish glass over time.

I was surprised at how shallow the bay was as the tide receded. Once the tide began to recede, it seemed to move very quickly. Much of the area that had been covered with water was now a large mudflat, and I found a wine bottle with a cap and a beer bottle. The wine bottle cap had been compromised by rust and had holes. It was from the Taylor Wine Company, which had started in 1880 and was sold to Coca-Cola in 1977. Unfortunately, although it had a company name, the bottle did not have a date, but it was still interesting to find a semi-intact wine bottle on the beach. The beer bottle did not have a cap or a name, but it was still an intact bottle.

It would be a very good idea to visit this beach during low tide early in the morning, especially after a storm, to see what washes up. Any sea glass that washes ashore is undoubtedly spotted and quickly collected by other sea glass hunters, and this beach gets picked over very quickly.

Reference: Heintzelman and Snell, 1974

9. Chesapeake & Delaware Canal Belemnites and *Exogyra* Oysters

The spoil piles are just east of the Reedy Point Bridge.

See map page 29.
County: New Castle
Site type: Dredge spoils
Land status: Reportedly administered by US Army Corps of Engineers
Material: Belemnites and *Exogyra* oysters
Host rock: Spoil piles of Upper Cretaceous Mount Laurel Formation
Difficulty: Easy
Family-friendly: Yes
Tools needed: Screen, shovel, gloves
Special concerns: Can be very hot in summer, ticks, heavy vegetation around piles

Special attractions: Ship watching along the C&D Canal, fishing
GPS parking: 39°33'35"N / 75°34'48"W
GPS Dredge Spoils: 39°33'42"N / 75°34'38"W
Topographic quadrangle: Delaware City, DE–NJ
Finding the site: From I-95, take exit 4A for DE 7 South. From DE 7 South, follow the signs for DE 1 South (Dover) and merge onto DE 1 South. Continue about 4.9 miles and merge into US 13 South. Take exit 152 for US 13 South/DE 72 toward Delaware City/St. Georges. Keep left at the fork and follow the signs for DE 72/ US 13 South/DE 7/DE 9. Turn left onto 13 South, then make a slight left onto DE 72 South and onto DE 9 South. Follow DE 9 South for 2.3 miles. You will now be in Delaware City. This is where it gets a little tricky. Take the last exit to the right before getting onto the Reedy Point Bridge. This is Polktown Road. If you get on the Reedy Point Bridge, you have missed the turn onto Polktown Road. Continue south on Polktown Road for about 0.8 mile, and the road will end at the canal. Turn right (east), proceed under Reedy Point Bridge, and park at the base of a small inclined access road with a locked gate. The spoil piles are about 800 feet northeast of the gate.

Rockhounding

These belemnites and *Exogyra* oyster were found with just a few screens from the piles.

The Chesapeake & Delaware (C&D) Canal connects the Delaware River with Chesapeake Bay. The canal was started in the early 1800s and at the time was one of the most expensive canal projects ever undertaken. The swamps and marshes made for poor working conditions, and the soft, poorly consolidated Cretaceous sediments continually slid back into the ditch. Today the canal is 14 miles long, 450 feet wide, and 40 feet deep. It is owned and operated by the Philadelphia District of the US Army Corps of Engineers.

Like most canals, it is necessary to periodically dredge material from the ship channel. The spoil piles have been deposited on both sides of the canal

Screening is by far the best way to find fossils at this site.

over time, and the location of piles can be observed on air and satellite photos. Some of the these spoil piles contain fossils, and the principal spoil piles for fossil collecting are the piles just north of the canal and east of the Reedy Point Bridge. These piles contain sediments from the Upper Cretaceous Mount Laurel Formation and lots of fossils.

The piles can be seen if you drive over the Reedy Point Bridge and look east on the north side of the canal, and they are also easily seen on satellite photos. I visited the piles by myself in May and June of 2014, and came equipped with a shovel and a screen. During my first trip in May, I was able to quickly find fragments of belemnites, which are the elongated, torpedo-shaped orange to brown fossils that are nearly entirely composed of aragonite. They are about the thickness of a pencil and have a pointed end. Belemnites are also the state fossil of Delaware. At this site they are nearly all broken and generally found as short pieces that are ½ inch to a couple inches long. I also found a tooth-shaped fragment and several interesting oyster-like shells with a hooked "beak," which I later learned were *Exogyra*, an extinct saltwater bivalve often described as an oyster.

During my second trip I came with a small group that included my wife, sister-in-law, and another friend. We found that the long grasses and bushes had grown considerably since spring, and there were not any clear paths to get to the piles. We finally bushwhacked to a pile and found lots of belemnites but not many *Exogyra*, but unfortunately we were somewhat limited on time, as it was late in the day.

A few weeks later I returned by myself to the C&D Canal area to check other soil piles. By now the vegetation was extremely thick, and I could not access any of the piles that I spotted on the north side of the canal using Google Maps. I also tried to access the "Deep Cut," which is where the Cretaceous outcrops are exposed on the north side of the canal. I almost got stuck in slumping soils and eaten alive by bugs, and the tide was also not favorable. I did not find any fossils in the Deep Cut. I also checked the piles on the south side of the canal opposite the piles east of the Reedy Point Bridge. These were relatively easy to access, but I did not find any fossils there.

If you come to the C&D Canal, I suggest focusing on the piles east of the Reedy Point Bridge. With a little effort you will find lots of belemnites and likely some *Exogyra* oysters. If you do not have a shovel or screen, it is still worth visiting the piles if you are in the area. You will very likely find some loose belemnites, oysters, and other fossils on the surface of the piles if you simply use your eyes and watch the ground surface for pointed pieces and white shells.

Reference: Lauginiger, 1988

10. Odessa Petrified Wood

The best way to find the wood is to scan areas of disturbed ground, such as the borders of residential construction sites.

County: New Castle
Site type: Loose rocks on surface
Land status: Private, not posted
Material: Petrified wood
Host rock: Miocene Calvert Formation/Pleistocene Columbia Formation
Difficulty: Easy to moderate
Family-friendly: Yes
Tools needed: Hammer or other tool to pry rocks from ground
Special concerns: As area is constantly developed, sites will become harder to find
Special attractions: Delaware beaches to the south
GPS parking: 39°25'07"N / 75°38'46"W
Note: The petrified wood is found over a wide area.

Sites 10–12

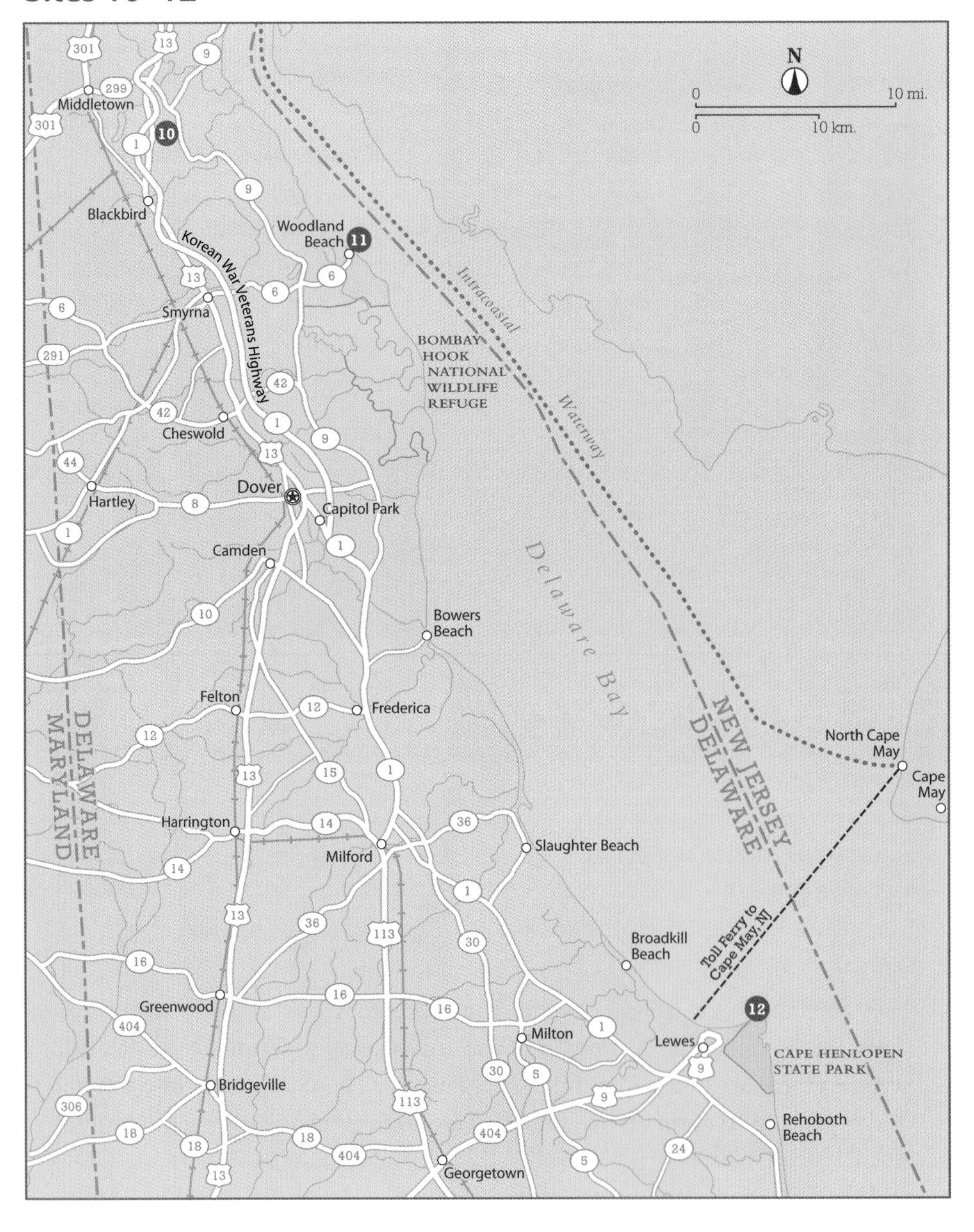

N
0
10 mi.
0
10 km.
Middletown
Blackbird
Woodland Beach
Korean War Veterans Highway
Smyrna
Intracoastal Waterway
BOMBAY HOOK NATIONAL WILDLIFE REFUGE
Cheswold
Dover
Hartley
Capitol Park
Camden
Delaware Bay
Bowers Beach
Felton
Frederica
DELAWARE
MARYLAND
NEW JERSEY
DELAWARE
North Cape May
Cape May
Harrington
Milford
Slaughter Beach
Toll Ferry to Cape May, NJ
Broadkill Beach
Greenwood
Milton
Lewes
CAPE HENLOPEN STATE PARK
Bridgeville
Rehoboth Beach
Georgetown

Topographic quadrangle: Middletown, DE

Finding the site: The locations for collecting petrified wood in the Odessa area change with time. The best way to find a suitable location is to check the satellite photos on Google Earth or a similar mapping service, and look for areas of recent construction where soils have been scraped up and exposed. Some of the most recent construction has been south of Odessa in new housing developments. To get to this area, head south on DE 1, which is a toll road, and take exit 142 toward US 13 South. When you reach Odessa, turn left (southeast) onto DE 299 and follow this south for approximately 1.8 miles. Turn left (southeast) onto Taylors Bridge Road (Route 9) and follow this about 1.8 miles, then turn right (west) onto Fieldsboro Road. At the time of this writing (summer 2014), this location had several areas of new housing construction and excavated soils. Look for areas where new houses are being built with freshly exposed soils, but stay out of any ground that is posted against trespassing.

Rockhounding

The Odessa area is well known for petrified wood that can found on the ground surface. The bedrock of the area is mapped as Miocene Calvert Formation, but the petrified wood is reportedly found in the overlying sediments of the Pleistocene Columbia Formation. This region is extremely flat, and identifying bedrock formations is complicated due to the lack of exposures and constant development.

This flat piece of petrified wood has a small knot and was found lying on the ground surface.

The key is to find a location that is open to collecting. When we visited the locality in June 2014, we were able to find an area that had been partially cleared, and it did not have any posted signs against access. It was obvious that many people also used the area for walking their dogs and short hikes. We parked at the coordinates listed in the "GPS parking" section above and hiked around the area, scanning the ground for petrified wood. It is not easy to find. We found lots of pebbles and sand, and finally found some pieces of petrified wood. Just before leaving I found a nice flat piece with a knot. You do not need to break any rocks, but it may be helpful to bring a hammer, chisel, or flat-bladed screwdriver to pry rocks from the ground.

Unfortunately, by the time you read this, this site may be a house or a street. This is a constantly evolving locality and with time may ultimately vanish. In the meantime, it should be relatively easy to find new locations in the region to search with the easy access to recent satellite photos. Alternatively you can simply drive around and look for barren ground that has been exposed during construction of developments. Some of the regional mineral clubs sometimes obtain permission to hunt in farm fields near Odessa, and these would be excellent trips to take if you get the opportunity.

Reference: Pickett and Spoljaric, 1971

11. Woodland Beach Sea Glass

Woodland Beach is very rocky and not good for swimming, but it is good for polishing sea glass.

See map page 56.

County: New Castle
Site type: Beach
Land status: Public
Material: Sea glass
Host rock: Beach sediments
Difficulty: Easy
Family-friendly: Yes
Tools needed: Container to collect glass
Special concerns: Lots of sharp glass, muddy water
Special attractions: Fishing along beach
GPS parking: 39°19'54"N / 75°28'16"W
Topographic quadrangle: Bombay Hook Island, DE–NJ

Finding the site: From US 13 South, take DE 6 East and follow it about 8.1 miles. This then turns into Beach Avenue. The parking area will then be to your left. Woodland Beach is right in front of the parking area.

Rockhounding

Woodland Beach was once a thriving summer resort with ferry service between Wilmington and Delaware. The area was most active in the late 1800s and early 1900s. This provided a steady stream of glass bottles and ceramics from trash dumping, ferry users, and local boaters throwing their empty wine and liquor bottles overboard. In 1914 a huge storm wiped out the only road to Woodland Beach, and afterwards the town suffered a dramatic decrease in tourists and was never again a big tourist destination.

Today Woodland Beach is one of the last relatively undeveloped waterfronts in Delaware. The area is now part of the Woodland Beach Wildlife Management Area. The abundance of nearby wetlands and the steadily encroaching shoreline make it a difficult area to develop, and it is out of the

Some parts of Woodland Beach are pebbly and full of glass shards, which have not yet been polished enough to be considered sea glass.

way with respect to many beaches, so it will likely remain undeveloped for a while. Another aspect that keeps development at bay is the abundance of broken glass and rocks on the beach. While not good for swimmers, it makes for good sea glass hunting.

We visited the beach in June 2014, but unfortunately got there after low tide had passed, and the water was rapidly rising as we walked along the beach. This was one of the first beaches we had ever visited for sea glass, and we were not really sure how best to look for it. We found an abundance of glass but much of it was as shards; however, I am sure that we could have had better success if we had arrived at low tide. I was surprised at the number of kids and adults that swam in the water with all of the broken glass. Many other collectors have visited this beach and it is undoubtedly picked over, so it is best to come at low tide after a storm. It has many of the characteristics of a great sea glass beach, such as a long history of settlement and a pebbly shoreline that gets lots of wave action, and we plan to visit it again during low tide.

Reference: Hansen, 2013

12. Cape Henlopen Beach Quartz

The beach at this site is extremely calm, as it is shielded from the main waves by Cape Henlopen.

See map page 56.
County: Sussex
Site type: Beach
Land status: Cape Henlopen State Park
Material: Quartz pebbles and fossil coral
Host rock: Beach sand
Difficulty: Easy
Family-friendly: Yes
Tools needed: None
Special concerns: State park often has shoreline access restrictions
Special attractions: Bird watching, swimming
GPS parking: 38°47'43"N / 75°05'30"W
Topographic quadrangle: Cape Henlopen, DE–NJ

Finding the site: Take DE 1 South, which is the main route to the Delaware beaches. Turn left (northeast) onto US 9 East and go about 2.7 miles. Turn right onto Cape Henlopen Drive and follow the signs into Cape Henlopen State Park. There is a fee to enter the park. Cape Henlopen Drive turns into Engineer Road, and after you enter the park, turn left onto Dune Road and go 0.2 mile. Turn right onto Post Lane, go about 0.7 mile, and turn left onto Post Road. Follow this for 0.7 mile to the parking area at Cape Henlopen Point. The beach with the quartz pebbles is to your left (west) and is on the west side of the cape.

Rockhounding

Cape Henlopen State Park is the large cape on the east coast of Delaware where the Atlantic Ocean converges with Delaware Bay. The cape is a huge sand dune that is steadily migrating north. The windward (east) side of the cape has lots of surf, sand, and rough waves, while the leeward (west) side is shielded by the cape and has very little waves. This makes the leeward side a good, safe place for beachcombing, especially with smaller kids.

The beach on the west side of the cape has semi-clear quartz pebbles, and many of these are similar to "Cape May diamonds." Cape May diamonds are clear quartz pebbles that become very clear when properly tumbled and polished. Fragments of fossil coral can also be found. At the time of my visit, which was late on a Friday afternoon in June 2014, there were at least two families with small children looking for shells, coral, and anything else that would catch their eye. It seemed like a very pleasant and safe beach, especially for kids.

Well-rounded quartz pebbles and fossil coral can be found along the shoreline.

The west side of the cape was in great contrast to the beaches on the east side of the cape. The east-side beaches had very large waves, and the surf was quite rough. However, from a beachcombing perspective, these beaches were nearly entirely sand and did not have any significant quartz pebbles or other types of rocks.

It is also worth noting that much of the western beach on the cape is closed to access during the piping plover nesting season. This closure is from March to

September, and it is critical to protect these shorebirds. You must make certain to stay out of these areas when closed, but fortunately the rest of the beach is quite extensive and you should still be able to find lots of semi-clear quartz pebbles in the areas that remain open for access.

Reference: Ramsey, 2003

MARYLAND

Kilgore Falls, northern Maryland (Site 24). Maryland has a wide diversity of geologic terrains and has abundant rockhounding opportunities for both mineral and fossil collectors.

Maryland

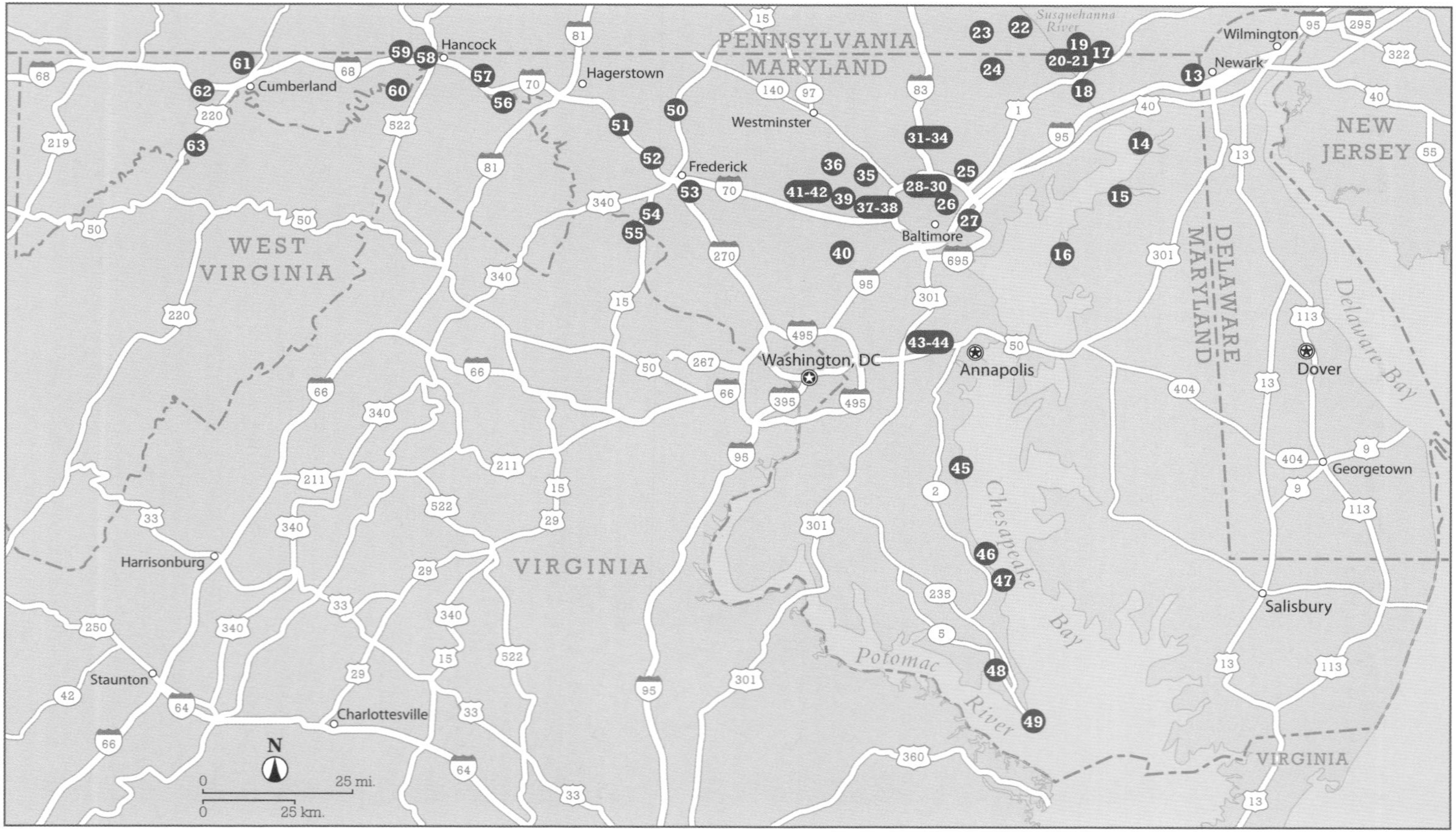

PENNSYLVANIA
MARYLAND
DELAWARE
MARYLAND
NEW JERSEY
WEST VIRGINIA
VIRGINIA
Susquehanna River
Delaware Bay
Chesapeake Bay
Potomac River
Wilmington
Newark
Hancock
Hagerstown
Cumberland
Westminster
Frederick
Baltimore
Washington, DC
Annapolis
Dover
Georgetown
Salisbury
Harrisonburg
Staunton
Charlottesville
N
0 25 mi.
0 25 km.

13. Big Elk Creek Orange Feldspar

The best places to find orange feldspar is in the small banks of rock along the creek banks.

County: Cecil
Site type: Stream rocks
Land status: Uncertain, not posted, but has fishing access
Material: Orange feldspar
Host rock: Port Deposit gneiss
Difficulty: Easy
Family-friendly: No; access to area is slightly challenging
Tools needed: Hammer
Special concerns: Poison ivy, mosquitoes, briars
Special attractions: Fishing along Big Elk Creek
GPS parking: 39°40'04"N / 75°49'30"W
GPS feldspar area: 39°40'02"N / 75°49'32"W
Topographic quadrangle: Newark West, DE–MD–PA
Finding the site: From I-95, take exit 109B for MD 279 North. Go northeast about 0.8 mile and turn left (west) onto MD 277 West, which is Fletchwood Road. Go

west for 1.3 miles and turn right (north) onto Appleton Road. Continue 0.9 mile and turn left (west) onto Brewster Bridge Road. In about 0.7 mile you will cross Big Elk Creek. Cross the creek and make a U-turn, then park on the shoulder on the south side of the road just east of the bridge. This is apparently the parking area used for fishing access. Parking is very limited. From here you can walk to the creek, and the feldspar is found in the loose rocks along the creek.

Rockhounding

Big Elk Creek cuts through a thick section of early Paleozoic Port Deposit gneiss. Nearly all of the land in the area is private, and this locality is one of the few places where you can safely park and enter Big Elk Creek. Most of the rocks in the creek are weathered gneisses and quartzites, but you can find some large pieces of orange feldspar that often shows excellent cleavage and is a light orange when broken.

The best rocks that I found were just south of the bridge, and I accessed the area by approaching from the west. The area was very overgrown and did not have any trails to speak of, and as it was summer, I had to fight my way through many spiderwebs, which I have never enjoyed much. The area south of the bridge has a large bank that extends towards the middle of the creek and has many cobble-size rocks, and this is one of the better areas to see the rocks in this creek.

The large feldspar pieces in this bank likely represent feldspar-rich sections of pegmatites that formed in the Port Deposit gneiss. A minor amount of mica is found with some of the feldspar as well. I kept my eyes open for tourmaline or other minerals that might have also formed in the pegmatites, but did not see any significant minerals other than the orange feldspar. This site is obviously best visited during low water, and I highly recommend long pants and boots, as there are no good paths to the creek and the shoreline is largely briars, stinging nettle, and other painful plants to hike through.

Look for orange rocks that are subangular, which is indicative of the internal crystal structure of the feldspar.

Reference: Cleaves et al., 1968

Sites 13–14

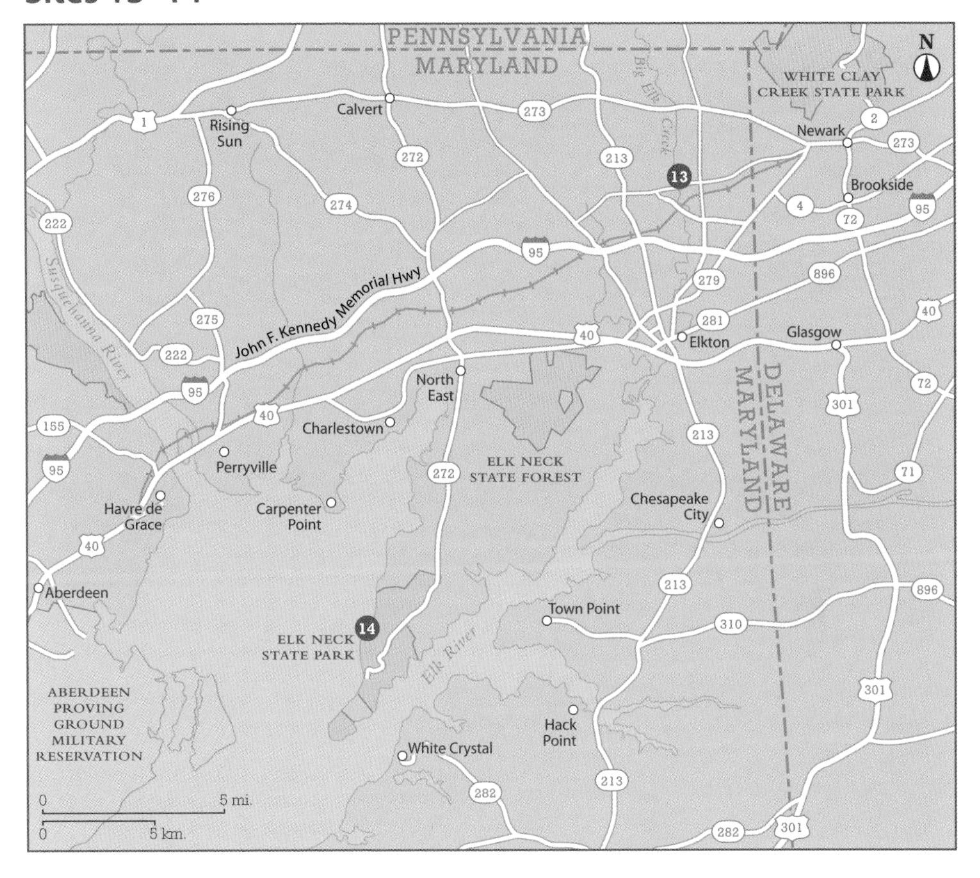

PENNSYLVANIA
MARYLAND
N
WHITE CLAY CREEK STATE PARK
Big Elk Creek
Rising Sun
Calvert
Newark
Brookside
John F. Kennedy Memorial Hwy
Susquehanna River
Elkton
Glasgow
DELAWARE
MARYLAND
North East
Charlestown
Perryville
ELK NECK STATE FOREST
Havre de Grace
Carpenter Point
Chesapeake City
Aberdeen
Town Point
ELK NECK STATE PARK
Elk River
ABERDEEN PROVING GROUND MILITARY RESERVATION
Hack Point
White Crystal
0
5 mi.
0
5 km.

14. Elk Neck Hematitic Conglomerate

The best examples of the hematitic conglomerate are found at this rocky beach just west of North East Beach, which is seen in the background.

See map page 69.

County: Cecil

Site type: Beach rocks

Land status: Elk Neck State Park

Material: Hematitic conglomerate

Host rock: Cretaceous Potomac Group sediments

Difficulty: Easy

Family-friendly: Yes

Tools needed: None; collecting not allowed

Special concerns: Water at beach can be dirty, rocks may be obscured during high tides

Special attractions: Hike to Elk Neck lighthouse, fishing and swimming on beach

GPS parking: 39°29'37"N / 75°59'16"W
GPS beach with rocks: 39°29'22"N / 75°59'27"W
Topographic quadrangle: Earleville, MD
Finding the site: From I-95, take the exit for MD 272 South. Go about 11.3 miles and turn right (west) onto North East Beach Road. You will then have to pay a fee to enter the park. Continue about 1.2 miles to the parking area, and the beach is just northwest of the parking area.

Rockhounding

This is an interesting site that was found by my wife, Rosalina, during an outing with her friends. She brings home driftwood like I bring home rocks, and driftwood collecting is legal at Elk Neck State Park. She had noticed the heavy brown rocks on the beach when driftwood collecting and thought they were very interesting. We visited the site together in May 2014. The area that she collected driftwood at is west of the North East Beach, which is one of the area's main swimming beaches.

Elk Neck State Park requires an entrance fee per person, and it is higher if you are not a Maryland resident. We parked at the parking area and walked to North East Beach, which is very close. The area just west of the beach becomes rocky and you do not want to walk here barefoot, so if you are visiting the beach, be sure to put on your shoes before you walk out to the rocks. The rocky part of the beach is strewn with large rocks of the Cretaceous Patapsco Group, and these are mainly sediments that range from sandstone to very coarse, poorly sorted

The hematitic conglomerate sometimes has a botryoidal texture.

conglomerate. Many of the rocks are very dense and high in iron, and some of them resemble bog iron ores.

The most interesting-looking rocks are the hematitic conglomerates with a botryoidal texture on the surface. These rocks are often dark purple and very heavy. Many people simply refer to them as ironstones. Unfortunately, as this is a Maryland state park, no collecting of rocks is allowed, so you can only enjoy looking at these conglomerates. However, feel free to take some driftwood.

Reference: Cleaves et al., 1968

15. Betterton Beach Sea Glass

Betterton Beach is generally sandy, and sea glass can be found throughout the beach.

County: Kent
Site type: Beach
Land status: Kent County Parks and Recreation
Material: Sea glass
Host rock: Beach sands
Difficulty: Easy
Family-friendly: Yes
Tools needed: None
Special concerns: Beach limited in size
Special attractions: Swimming on beach
GPS parking: 39°22'13"N / 76°03'49"W
GPS beach: 39°22'17"N / 76°03'47"W
Topographic quadrangle: Betterton, MD

Finding the site: From US 301 South, take MD 290 South and proceed about 4 miles. In the town of Galena, this turns into MD 213 South. Continue 5.7 miles west and take a slight right onto MD 298 West. Continue 2.6 miles and take the fork to the right (northwest) onto MD 566. Go 1.2 miles, and this turns into MD 292 North. Go 0.8 mile and keep to the right to stay on MD 292 North. Go 2.8 miles into the town of Betterton and turn left (west) onto Ericsson Avenue. Park in the parking area on the left side of Ericsson Avenue and walk north to Betterton Beach.

Rockhounding

Betterton is one of numerous cities on Chesapeake Bay that claim the title of "Jewel of the Chesapeake." Even if it is not the only jewel, Betterton is still a very scenic town and deserves the name. The Betterton area was first settled in the late 1600s, and in 1715 a small fishing village, known as Crews Landing, was established. This later became a port for shipping local farm produce to urban markets. When the Chesapeake & Delaware Canal was built, Betterton became an important stop for boats using the canal, and the steamboats brought economic growth to the town. In the late 1800s there were as many as eleven scheduled steamboat landings daily at Betterton.

These pieces of glass are frosted, but the angular character suggests they are relatively recent glasses.

The town soon became a booming beach resort, and it flourished from after World War I to the start of the Great Depression. Restaurants, taverns, dance halls, bowling alleys, and amusement arcades all helped create Betterton's resort image. Sadly, like most beach resorts on the Chesapeake, the town began to decline after the Depression started, and the building of bridges to connect Baltimore with ocean beach cities further reduced the tourists that came to Betterton. Today the town is much smaller but still has a good public beach.

Since the town goes back to the late 1600s and was a steamboat stop/beach resort from the late 1800s to the early 1930s, it has lots of potential for sea glass. The beach has a fair amount of sand but also a large amount of pebbles and rocks, and sea glass can be found along the shoreline. We came as high tide was approaching, and there were others on the beach looking for glass as well. We found a fair amount of white and green glass, but some of it was still shard-like. The beach gets picked over quite a bit; it is recommended to visit it at low tide, and try to be the first one on the beach.

References: Maryland Historic Trust, 1984

Sites 15–16

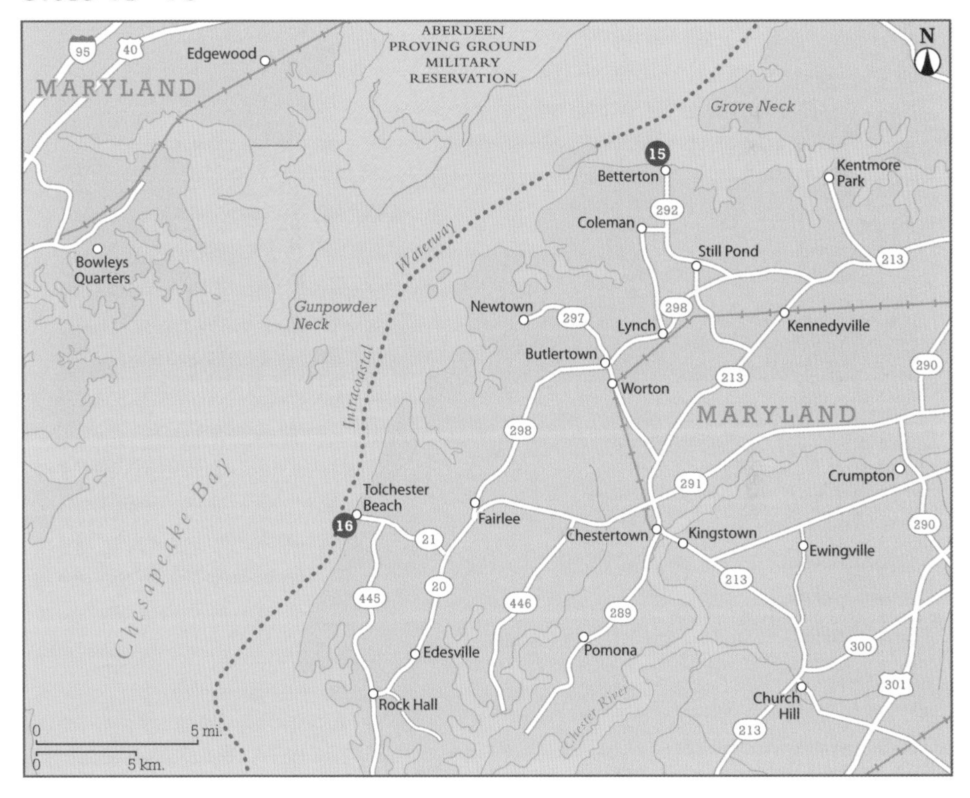

16. Tolchester Beach Sea Glass

Tolchester Beach is easy to walk on, and you can find sea glass fairly quickly.

See map page 75.

County: Kent
Site type: Beach
Land status: Public beach, private parking
Material: Sea glass
Host rock: Beach sand
Difficulty: Easy
Family-friendly: Yes
Tools needed: None
Special concerns: Parking can be an issue, private property near beach
Special attractions: None; this is a very remote area
GPS parking: 39°12'48"N / 76°14'39"W
GPS beach: 39°12'58"N / 76°14'37"W

Topographic quadrangle: Rock Hall, MD

Finding the site: From the Chesapeake Bay Bridge, head east on US 301 North to exit 37. Turn left (northwest) onto MD 405 North and go 2.6 miles. Turn left (northwest) onto MD 19 West and go 1 mile to the town of Church Hill, then turn right (northeast) and continue on MD 19. Go 1.1 miles and turn right onto MD 213 (northwest). Continue 6.1 miles to Kingstown, turn left (southwest) onto North Cross Street, and take the second right onto High Street. Go 0.9 mile, come to a traffic circle, and take the second exit onto MD 20 West. Follow MD 20 West for 7 miles and turn right onto MD 21/Tolchester Beach Road. Take this 3.3 miles to Tolchester Beach. It may be possible to park at the marina, but if not, you should be able to park at the end of Tolchester Beach Road near the boat-launching area and walk to the beach, provided you do not block access for boats or vehicles.

Rockhounding

Tolchester Beach, located on the eastern side of Chesapeake Bay, was a popular tourist resort from the late 1800s to the early 1960s. An amusement park opened at Tolchester Beach in 1877, and the town became a popular destination to escape Baltimore during the summer. In addition to the Baltimore ferries, Tolchester Beach was served by steamship traffic along the bay, and at its peak the town received 20,000 visitors during summer weekends. However, the opening of the Chesapeake Bay Bridge in 1952 all but wiped out the ferry traffic, and the park was closed by 1962.

Rounded and roughly polished sea glass can be found on the rocky parts of the beach.

When the amusement park first opened, the management announced that the resort would be under strict temperance management, and that no alcohol would be allowed on the ferry. Like many similar amusement parks and beaches of the day, the park was segregated and was mainly for middle-class white families from Baltimore. Garbage, including bottles, porcelain tiles, dishes, glasses, and other debris and trash associated with the amusement park and town, was undoubtedly dumped into Chesapeake Bay.

Despite the lack of liquor, wine, and beer bottles that would have been dumped offshore had more alcohol been consumed, lots of glass still washes onto the beach. During our visit to the area, there was another couple looking for sea glass, and they collected at least two handfuls of polished white and green glass with a few blue pieces. We got there just after low tide, and while we found several good pieces, I think the best were already picked up by previous hunters that day.

The best glass seems to be to the north end of the beach where it becomes rocky. Be sure to stay off the private land just off the beach. In Maryland the property line starts at the high tide mark, so if you go during low tide and stay on the beach, you should be able to avoid private property. The beach appears to have steady wave action from the eastward-trending winds, and the pebbly and rocky shoreline helps to polish the glass. Tolchester Beach, unfortunately, also reportedly has high levels of bacteria, so it is not a good beach for swimming, but you also do not want to swim at a beach that is principally rocks and glass.

References: Holly, 1994; Usilton, 2010; Maryland State Archives, n.d.

17. Octoraro Creek Serpentine

Serpentine can be found in the rocks placed next to the bridge as well as in Octoraro Creek.

See map on page 83.

County: Cecil

Site type: Stream rocks and riprap

Land status: Private, not posted

Material: Serpentine

Host rock: Serpentine

Difficulty: Moderate

Family-friendly: Yes

Tools needed: None, but hammer is useful for trimming

Special concerns: Land status, traffic

Special attractions: Fishing in Octoraro Creek

GPS parking: 39°42'24"N / 76°06'56"W

Topographic quadrangle: Rising Sun, MD–PA

Finding the site: From US 1, turn north onto Horseshoe Road and proceed approximately 1.3 miles. At the intersection with Octoraro Creek, cross the one-lane bridge and park at the fishing access to the left on the west side of the creek. From here you can walk directly down to Octoraro Creek.

Rockhounding

Octoraro Creek is one of the principal drainages for the ultramafic rocks along the Maryland-Pennsylvania border. Virtually all the land in the region is private, and this creek offers one of the only localities to see the rocks of the region up close. I have been to the area twice, and unfortunately both times the water was relatively high. I was able to find some pieces of serpentine rocks in Octoraro Creek, but they were not as abundant as I expected. I found much more serpentine on the east bank just south of the bridge where quarried rocks have been placed between the road and creek. This area is overgrown with briars and poison ivy, and many of the rocks are unstable, so be very careful if you walk around here to look at the serpentine.

Some of the serpentine exhibit light purple as well as green banding.

The parking area is also covered with crushed stone from the local quarries, and small pieces of green serpentine can be found on the ground in this area. Many of these pieces are elongated and waxy, but I did not find any that I would consider to represent williamsite, which is the bright apple-green variety of antigorite that is found in some of the ultramafic rocks along the state line. It might be worthwhile to explore farther upstream, especially during low water, but you have to make certain that you do not trespass on private land.

References: Cleaves et al., 1968

18. Conowingo Dam Area River Rocks

Conowingo Dam is a very large dam, and the beach is crowded with fishermen when the water is low.

See map page 83.
County: Harford
Site type: Rocks along stream bank
Land status: Public fishing access
Material: Serpentine
Host rock: Baltimore Gabbro Complex rocks
Difficulty: Easy
Family-friendly: Yes
Tools needed: None
Special concerns: Water levels occasionally are too high
Special attractions: Fishing for striped bass at dam
GPS parking: 39°39'17"N / 76°10'23"W

GPS shoreline near dam: 39°39'21"N / 76°10'28"W
Topographic quadrangle: Conowingo Dam, MD–PA
Finding the site: From US 1 North, proceed east towards the Susquehanna River. As you near the dam, turn right onto Shuresville Road, go 0.7 mile, and then make a sharp left onto Shureslanding Road. Go 0.7 mile to the Susquehanna River, turn left, and continue 0.3 mile to the parking area.

Rockhounding

Serpentine with banding can be found in the rocks on the rocky shore downstream of the dam.

Conowingo Dam was built in 1928, and it is one of the largest non-federal hydroelectric dams in the country. The dam is located near the contact of the Baltimore Gabbro Complex, Wissahickon schist, quartz-diorite gneiss, and Port Deposit gneiss. Some of the rocks used for riprap and crushed stone for parking areas came from local quarries, and some interesting serpentine rocks and minerals can be seen along the riverbanks and parking areas.

This site offers an opportunity to look for polished rocks along the rocky beach just south of the dam, serpentine and gneissic rocks in the riprap along the riverbank, and waxy green elongated serpentine in the crushed stone of some of the parking areas. During my first visit to the dam in April 2014, the water level was too high and much of the dam area was closed. Our looking for rocks was mainly along the river trail south of the parking area, and some of the most interesting pieces I found were a few small waxy green serpentine pieces in the parking area.

When I returned in July 2014, the water levels were much lower. I came near twilight at the peak of a major bug hatch, and I was covered with unidentified non-biting flies. I was able to walk along a very rocky beach where several fishermen were fishing for striped bass. I looked closely at the large riprap boulders and saw a lot of coarse gneiss with some minor pegmatitic zones, but not much serpentine. I then looked at the rocks that were being washed up by waves along the shoreline, and discovered that several attractive green rocks could be found. Most of these were fine-grained serpentine rocks that had interesting patterns from the largely parallel orientation of dark minerals. Unfortunately it soon became dark. I was the only one looking for rocks, so at this site you will have to compete with fishermen as opposed to other rockhounds. Not surprisingly, the fishermen showed absolutely no interest in what I was doing.

Reference: Cleaves et al., 1968

Sites 17–21

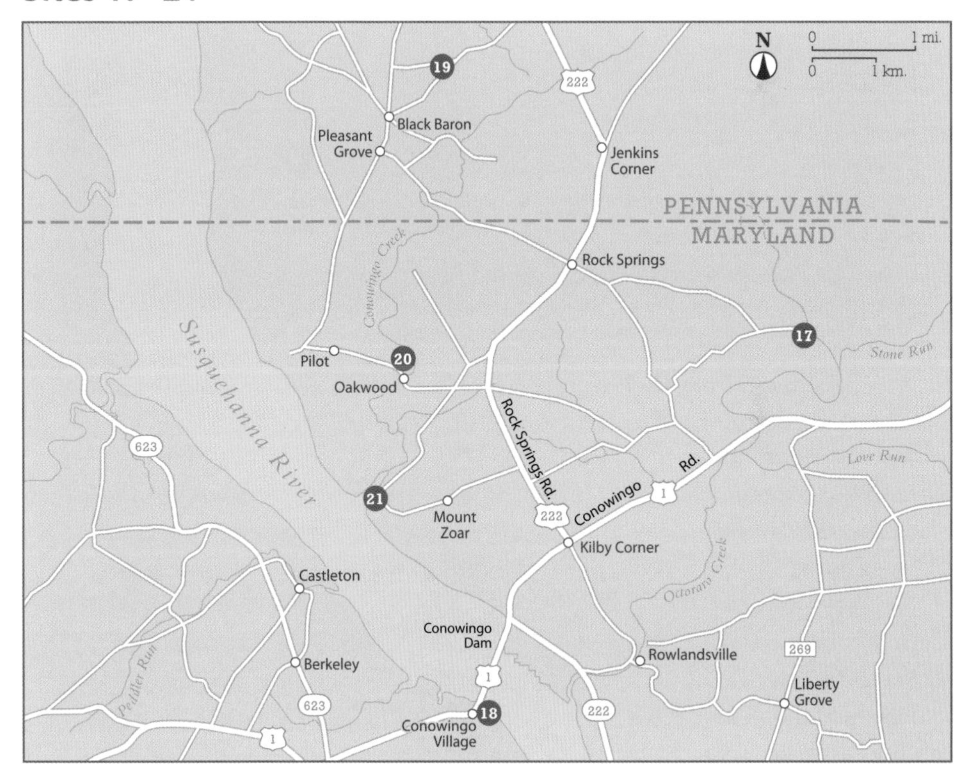

19. Black Barren Road Serpentine

This outcrop is one of the best roadside exposures of serpentine in the region.

See map page 83.
County: Lancaster, PA
Site type: Roadcut
Land status: Private, but may be in road right-of-way
Material: Lizardite
Host rock: Precambrian serpentine
Difficulty: Easy
Family friendly: Yes
Tools needed: None
Special concerns: Land status, no hammering or digging
Special attractions: Nottingham County Park Serpentine Barrens
GPS parking: 39°44'32"N / 76°10'50"W
Topographic quadrangle: Conowingo Dam, MD–PA

Finding the site: From US 1 North in Maryland, turn left (north) onto US 222 North. Continue 3.3 miles, and you will then cross into Pennsylvania. Continue another 2.4 miles and turn left onto Black Barren Road. Continue about 1 mile and look for the long greenish-gray outcrop on the right (north) side of the road. There is no parking here, and the only parking that I found was on the south side of the road in the shoulder opposite the outcrop.

Rockhounding

The serpentine is generally dark gray to green and has abundant lizardite at this outcrop.

This is one of the best roadcut exposures of serpentine in the Pennsylvania-Maryland region, and it is included in this guidebook since it is so close to the Maryland state line. I first saw this roadcut many years ago when traveling along Black Barren Road in southern Lancaster County, and I was impressed at the size of the roadcut and the prominent green to gray-green color of the serpentine. Unfortunately it is on private land, but a significant portion of the exposed serpentine rocks are adjacent to Black Barren Road and may be within the road right-of-way.

When my wife and I visited this roadcut in May 2014, the ground adjacent to the north side of the road at the roadcut was not posted against trespassing, while areas farther to the west and east were posted. We were able to park our car on the south side of Black Barren Road for a brief look at the outcrop and the associated serpentine minerals. Most of the serpentine appeared to be lizardite, which has a green scaly appearance. Some of the serpentine had waxy, slickensided surfaces, but most of the rocks were simply dark green to gray and weathered. I did not see any zones of white chrysotile or fibrous minerals, or any indications of apple-green williamsite. Plants do not grow well in the serpentine, and the name "Black Barren" is especially appropriate for this road.

Reference: Jones et al., 2006

20. Conowingo Creek–Pilot Road Serpentine

Serpentine can be found in the creek and in some of the rocks placed alongside the bridge for bank stabilization.

See map page 83.

County: Cecil

Site type: Streambed and bank rocks

Land status: Private, but not posted

Material: Serpentine

Host rock: Serpentinite

Difficulty: Moderate

Family-friendly: No; limited area, access questionable

Tools needed: Hammer

Special concerns: Land status uncertain

Special attractions: Fishing in Conowingo Creek

GPS parking: 39°42'02"N / 76°11'21"W

Topographic quadrangle: Conowingo Dam, MD–PA

Finding the site: From US 1 North, cross the Susquehanna River at Conowingo Dam and proceed 0.9 mile to the intersection with US 222 North, then turn left (north). Go 1.7 miles and turn left onto Old Conowingo Road. Go 0.3 mile and continue straight to get onto Pilot Town Road. Continue 0.6 mile to where Conowingo Creek crosses Pilot Town Road. Park at the shoulder on the north side of the creek, on the west side of Pilot Town Road, and walk to the creek.

Rockhounding

Conowingo Creek is one of the main drainages of the area of ultramafic rocks along the Maryland-Pennsylvania border. The bedrock of the area as Conowingo Creek approaches the Susquehanna is mapped as the Baltimore Gabbro Complex, which is largely composed of gabbroic rocks and does not have serpentine.

This piece had a section of a light translucent green mineral.

I had hoped to find some good pieces of serpentine and possibly some green williamsite, which is a type of antigorite that is highly prized by many collectors. We parked on the north side of Conowingo Creek and walked along the bank on both sides. The area upstream (east) of the bridge has some large banks of rocks, but most of these were very small and I did not see any interesting pieces of serpentine here. Downstream (west) along the south bank I found some good pieces of serpentine, but no williamsite. The south side of the creek just west of the bridge has a lot of quarried rocks that were used for bank stabilization, and many of these have some banded serpentine. We were able to find some light green serpentine that had slight translucent green mineralization, but did not find any pieces that I would call williamsite. Unfortunately our time was limited, and with more time we may have been able to find pieces with williamsite.

Reference: Cleaves et al., 1968

21. Conowingo Boat Landing Schist and Micaceous Granitic Rock

The schist float and granitic outcrop are upstream of this waterfall.

See map page 83.

County: Cecil

Site type: Outcrops along steep tributary to Conowingo Creek

Land status: Boat landing managed by Exelon Generation

Material: Fine-grained mica schist and micaceous pegmatite

Host rock: Baltimore Gabbro Complex

Difficulty: Easy

Family-friendly: No; tributary rocks are steep and slippery

Tools needed: Hammer

Special concerns: Rocks very slippery, collecting status uncertain

Special attractions: Fishing at Conowingo boat landing

GPS parking: 39°41'01"N / 76°11'43"W

GPS schist and pegmatite: 39°41'01"N / 76°11'37"W
Topographic quadrangle: Conowingo Dam, MD–PA
Finding the site: From US 1 North, cross the Susquehanna River at Conowingo Dam and proceed 0.9 mile to the intersection with US 222 North, then turn left (north). Go 0.9 mile and turn left (west) onto Mt. Zoar Road. Go 1.5 miles, and Mt. Zoar Road turns slightly left and becomes Old Conowingo Road. The boat landing is on the left. Park here and walk upstream on Old Conowingo Road to a small waterfall, which is on the tributary with the schist and pegmatite. Walk up the tributary to the off-white outcrops of crumbling granitic rock, which will be on the left (east) side of the tributary.

Rockhounding

This site is within rocks mapped as part of the Baltimore Gabbro Complex, but the rocks of interest here are colorful fine-grained iron-stained mica schist and a weathered granitic outcrop with abundant muscovite mica. Most of the rocks in the steep tributary are dark gneisses, but you can find flat pieces of

The schist has copper-like sheen, and the white granitic rock is full of silvery muscovite.

fine-grained mica schist along the creek bed. This schist is different than many of the other schists I have seen in Maryland in that it is very fine-grained and has iron staining that gives it a copper-like sheen. The sheen is reddish brown to golden and is best seen when the rock is wet and in the sun. The presence of the fairly large flat pieces of schist in this area suggests that a local outcrop of this schist is not too far upstream. If it was transported much farther, the schist would likely have become much smaller and rounded, just like other weathered schists in regional drainages.

The micaceous granite occurs in a large weathered outcrop that is crumbly on the surface, but relatively intact pieces are present below the surface of the weathered rock. I originally thought this was a pegmatite, but the mica and feldspar crystals do not vary much in size, indicating that this is likely best described as a very coarse granitic rock. The feldspar is presumably albite, as it is white to light gray, and the mica is nearly all muscovite. I was surprised to see such an outcrop in a mafic complex, and this suggests that while it may not be a pegmatite, it might represent a late-stage felsic dike.

Reference: Cleaves et al., 1968

22. Whiteford Slate

The area has a lot of parking, as it is used by firetrucks to fill their water tanks.

County: Harford
Site type: Driveway to former quarry
Land status: Uncertain; may be municipal land, not posted
Material: Slate
Host rock: Ordovician Peach Bottom slate
Difficulty: Easy
Family-friendly: Yes, but site size is very limited
Tools needed: None; collecting limited to loose rocks
Special concerns: Land status uncertain, site size is very small
Special attractions: Rocks State Park, Palmer State Park
GPS parking: 39°42'58"N / 76°20'08"W
Topographic quadrangle: Delta, PA–MD
Finding the site: From US 1, turn onto MD 136 North and head 7.1 miles northwest towards Whiteford. When you reach Whiteford, turn right (east)

onto Main Street, go 0.7 mile, and turn right (southeast) onto the appropriately named Slate Ridge Road. Go about 0.2 mile and look for the turnout on the right (southwest) side of the road next to a fenced former quarry. Park here, and you can see the slate bedrock on the ground.

Rockhounding

The Whiteford area has several large former slate quarries, but unfortunately all of them are private and inaccessible without permission. This site is used by the local fire department to withdraw water from the former quarry. The quarry area is fenced and clearly marked "no trespassing," but the entrance area is underlain by slate and pieces of slate can be found on the ground. Most of these pieces are relatively small, but I found a few large flat ones. The slate is dark gray to black and is fairly smooth.

I did not encounter any problems when I stopped to look at the slate, but I would not be comfortable with bringing a large group or excavating large pieces of slate. I would also not dig holes in the parking area to look for slate, as any holes could be damaging to fire department vehicles and personnel that

Large flat pieces of slate can be found on the surface of the parking area outside the former quarry.

need to use the site for water. Although it is a very small area, it is still one of the only safe roadside stops that you can make in Maryland if you want to get out of your car and look closely at the slate.

Reference: Cleaves et al., 1968

Sites 22–24

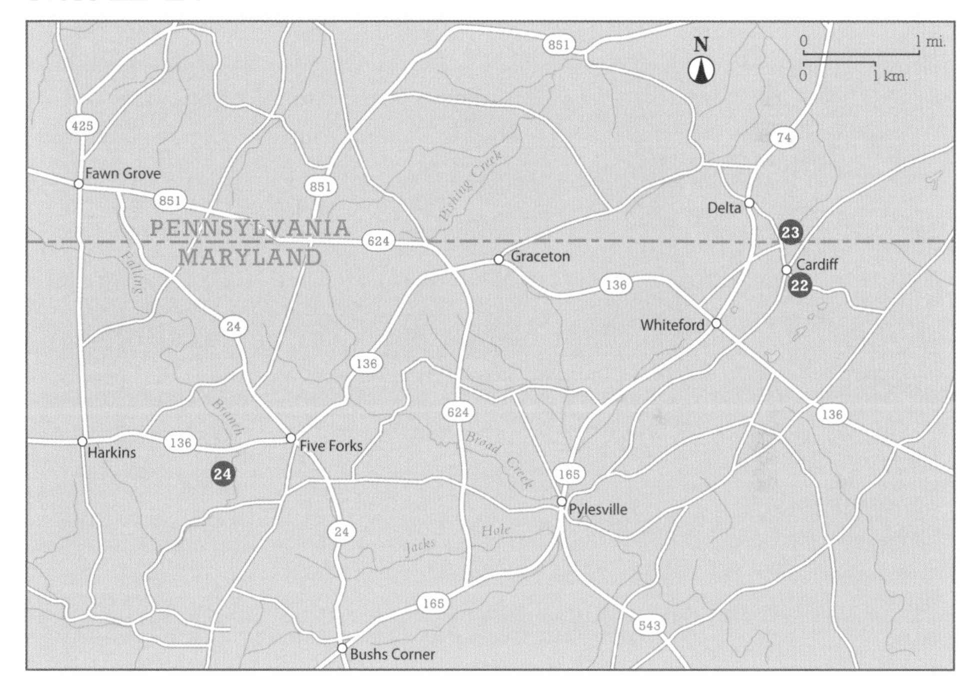

23. Cardiff Serpentine

This is a very small area of rocks, but they are very colorful and right next to the road.

See map page 93.

County: York, PA

Site type: Rock piles at bridge and stream

Land status: Private, not posted; may be in highway or stream right-of-way

Material: Serpentine

Host rock: Serpentine

Difficulty: Easy

Family-friendly: Yes, but limited space

Tools needed: None; no hammering should be done at this site

Special concerns: Site is next to road and businesses

Special attractions: Fishing at Conowingo Dam

GPS parking: 39°43'18"N / 76°20'12"W

Topographic quadrangle: Delta, PA–MD

Finding the site: From US 1, turn north onto MD 136 North and proceed 7.3 miles. Turn right (northeast) onto MD 165 North and go 0.6 mile. Bear right at the fork with Dooley Road and continue about 0.4 mile. You will now be in Pennsylvania. Cross over Scott Creek and park on the north shoulder of Dooley Road. The rocks are the riprap and stones that have been dumped along the east edge of Scott Creek on the south side of Dooley Road.

Rockhounding

This serpentine had a "tiger stripe" pattern.

This site is actually in Pennsylvania but is in this book since it nearly straddles the Maryland-Pennsylvania border. The area of Cardiff was known for "Verde Antique" serpentine, which has also been referred to as "green marble." Unfortunately all of the former quarries and mines are on private land and are not accessible to collectors except through special permission.

The quarry that produced the Verde Antique serpentine is fenced, and I scoured the area to see if I could find any accessible mine dumps or piles. Often the best place to look for accessible rocks in areas with limited access is along streams, and the topographic map of the area showed a very small drainage northeast of the quarry. We drove to this drainage and found that some serpentine rocks had been placed on the southeast side of the intersection of Scott Creek and Dooley Road. I was able to park on the north side of Dooley Road and walk across the street to the rock pile next to Scott Creek. This is a small pile, but fortunately it is very accessible and has some pieces of serpentine. It was not posted, and I did not have any trouble looking at the rocks.

One of the serpentine pieces that I found had an appearance that reminded me of tiger stripes. Some of the pieces also include dense black metallic minerals. Some of these rocks attract a magnet, indicating that magnetite is present, but the serpentine host rock suggests that some of the black metallic minerals may also include chromite. Since this is a small pile, it is best to limit collecting, and make sure that you do not compromise the integrity of the stream bank.

Reference: Pearre and Heyl, 1960

24. Kilgore Falls Pelitic Schist

The foliation in the pelitic schist is very prominent and can be seen in the exposures just east of the falls.

See map page 93.
County: Harford
Site type: Waterfall
Land status: Rocks State Park
Material: Pelitic schist
Host rock: Prettyboy schist
Difficulty: Easy
Family-friendly: Yes
Tools needed: None; collecting not allowed
Special concerns: Falling off falls and cliffs
Special attractions: Fishing at Conowingo Dam
GPS parking: 39°41'24"N / 76°25'22"W
GPS falls: 39°41'34"N / 76°25'37"W

Kilgore Falls is Maryland's second-highest free-falling waterfall.

Topographic quadrangle: Fawn Grove, PA–MD
Finding the site: From Bel Air, take MD 24 North for about 8.4 miles. Turn left (west) onto St. Mary's Road, go 0.4 mile, and continue on Clements Mill Road. Go about 400 feet and turn right (west) onto Falling Branch Road. Continue about 0.2 mile, and the parking area will be on your right. Park here and follow the trail to Kilgore Falls.

Rockhounding

Kilgore Falls is Maryland's second-highest free-falling waterfall. It is only 17 feet high, but the surrounding cliffs are higher, and it is a very impressive falls for the region. The area was privately owned and relatively unknown until it became part of the Rocks State Park system in 1993. The falls are now accessed by a trail from the parking area.

The falls are on Falling Branch, which is a tributary of Deer Creek. Falling Branch flows through Kilgore Rocks, which is a steep gorge that developed in the Prettyboy schist. The Prettyboy schist was previously known as the upper pelitic schist of the Precambrian Wissahickon Formation. The Wissahickon

Formation is mainly mica-chlorite schist produced from the metamorphism of fine-grained sandstones and shales. The Prettyboy schist was produced from the metamorphism of aluminum-rich clays and sandstones. This produced schist that is slightly finer-grained and higher in alumina content, and this provides the sheen of fine-grained muscovite on the rocks in the vicinity of the falls.

Although rock collecting is not allowed in the park, the bedrock exposures are well worth seeing. The outcrops around Kilgore Falls have intensely developed foliation, with a near vertical dip, and northeast–southwest trending strike. I am sure some hikers visit the falls and tell their kids or companions that these are striations from glaciation, as they somewhat resemble glacial scrapes, but this area was never glaciated. The schist is also interlayered with bands of quartz that parallel the foliation. In the creek the schist is very fine-grained and has a silvery appearance from muscovite mica, and slabs of silvery schist can be found in the creek as loose rocks.

The area has several trails around the falls, but the falls are left almost entirely in their natural state, and there are no barriers to keep people from slipping and falling off either the cliffs or the falls. If you are with small children, I highly recommend staying below the falls and away from the cliffs. The falls are best viewed from below, and the creek-bed mica is also best seen downstream of the falls.

References: Means, 1980; Southwick and Owens, 1968

25. Loch Raven Lower Dam Quarry Albite Pegmatites

This is the former quarry floor, and the pegmatites are found on the hillside of the north part of the former quarry.

County: Baltimore
Site type: Pegmatites in quarry
Land status: Baltimore County park
Material: Albite pegmatites
Host rock: Pegmatites that have intruded Cockeysville marble
Difficulty: Easy
Family-friendly: Yes, but some steep trails involved
Tools needed: None; collecting not allowed
Special concerns: Spiders, mosquitoes, ticks
Special attractions: Baltimore Inner Harbor
GPS parking: 39°25'30"N / 76°32'29"W
GPS trailhead to pegmatite: 39°25'31"N / 76°32'30"W

Topographic quadrangle: Towson, MD

Finding the site: From I-695 East, take exit 29A for Cromwell Bridge Road. Turn left (northeast) onto Cromwell Bridge Road, go 2.3 miles, and turn left (northwest) onto Loch Raven Drive. Go about 0.4 mile, and you will see the parking area to the left (west) and the lower dam to the right (east). The parking area is adjacent to a former quarry, and the pegmatite area is reached by a trail at the north end of the quarry.

Rockhounding

This large white albite feldspar crystal is typical of the size found in the pegmatites on the hillside.

The Lock Raven lower dam was built in 1881, and the upper dam was built in 1923. Loch Raven Reservoir is the main water supply for the city of Baltimore. The lower dam is easy to find, as it is the first dam upstream from the intersection of Cromwell Bridge Road and Loch Raven Drive. The parking area, which is used by kayakers, bicyclers, and sightseers, is next to a large open area which is the floor of a former quarry.

The main mass of the quarry is late Precambrian Cockeysville marble. During my first trip to the area, I looked for mineralization in the marble, but found it to be rather boring, and it was very difficult to climb on the slopes. During subsequent reviews of the literature, I learned that a large pegmatite body was present in the northern end of the quarry. The next time I came to the site, I went straight to the northern end and immediately found large off-white albite feldspar crystals in fine-grained granitic rocks. Many of the crystals were 2 to 3 inches long and a couple inches wide, and they showed excellent cleavage on broken surfaces.

The pegmatitic rocks and the feldspars are very abundant in this area. Mica and garnet are also reported, but I did not see any in the pegmatites or other rocks of the area. What I also encountered, unfortunately, was a lot of spiders. My trip was in late July 2014, and this must have been the peak of the spider season. Every time I tried to walk to an outcrop, I had to pass through webs with spiders. Fortunately my desire to see the albite feldspars overruled any fears that I had, but this could be a disturbing site if you cannot handle the frequent spiders. This site would likely be best to visit in the late fall or early spring when the vegetation is minimal and the insects and arachnids (i.e., spiders) are at a minimum. This is one of the best places I have found in the northeastern United States to see albite feldspars in pegmatite, and I highly recommend this stop for anyone who enjoys looking at interesting rocks in a very scenic area.

References: Cleaves, 1968; Edwards, 1987

Sites 25–30

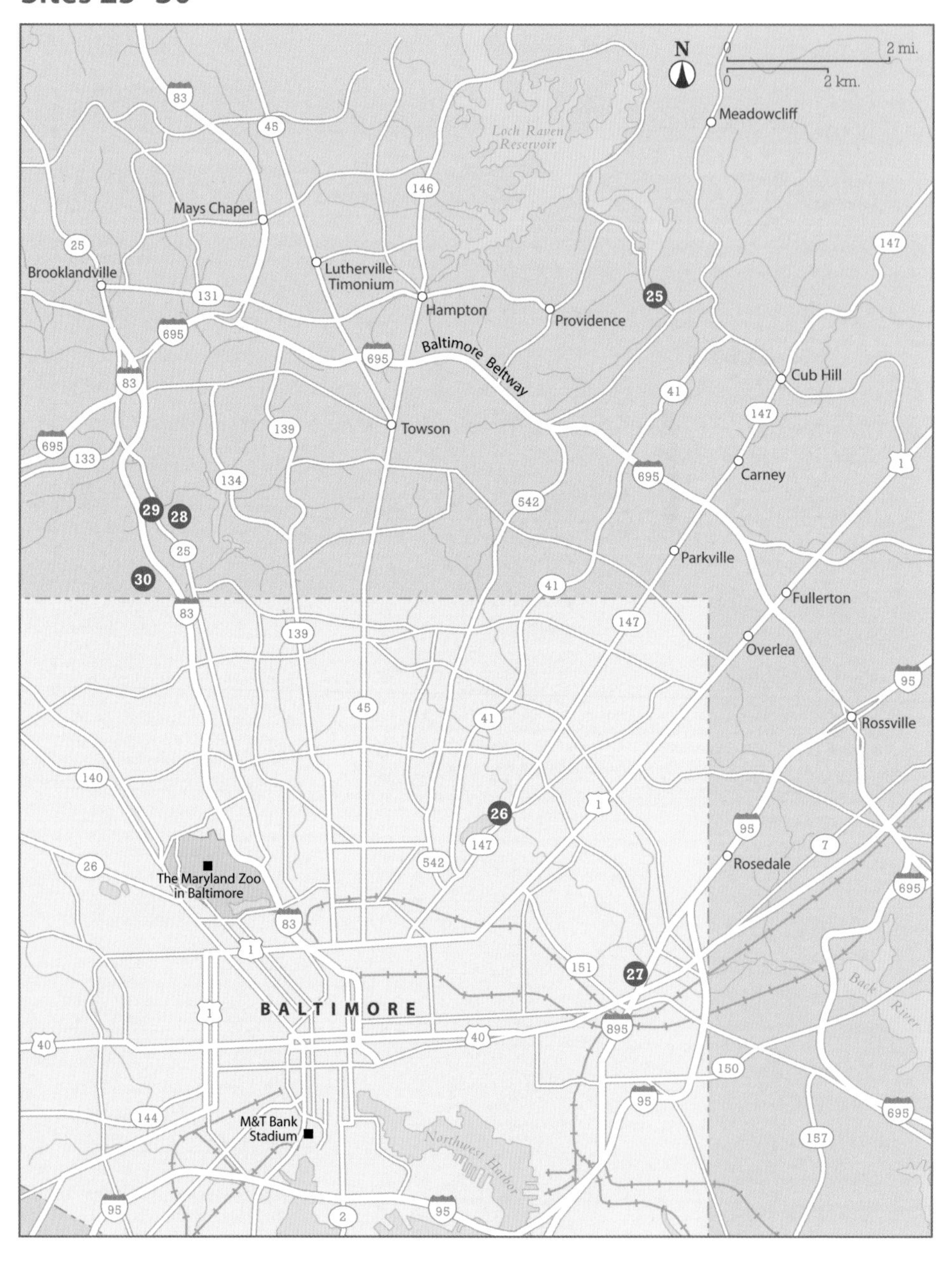

N
0
2 mi.
0
2 km.
Loch Raven Reservoir
Meadowcliff
Mays Chapel
Brooklandville
Lutherville-Timonium
Hampton
Providence
Baltimore Beltway
Cub Hill
Towson
Carney
Parkville
Fullerton
Overlea
Rossville
Rosedale
The Maryland Zoo in Baltimore
BALTIMORE
M&T Bank Stadium
Northwest Harbor
Back River
25
26
27
28
29
30

26. Herring Run Marble, Feldspar, and Tourmaline

Herring Run is loaded with rocks; the large white rocks are mainly marble.

See map page 102.

County: Baltimore
Site type: Streambed and adjacent rocks
Land status: City of Baltimore park
Material: White marble, orange feldspar, black tourmaline
Host rock: Various formations
Difficulty: Easy
Family-friendly: Yes
Tools needed: None; collecting not allowed
Special concerns: Polluted water in Herring Run
Special attractions: Baltimore Inner Harbor
GPS parking: 39°20'03"N / 76°34'36"W

GPS Herring Run: 39°20'04"N / 76°34'41"W
Topographic quadrangle: Baltimore East, MD
Finding the site: From I-695, take exit 31A for MD 147/Harford Road. Head southwest for about 4.2 miles, and when you pass the intersection with Argonne Drive, take the road to the right that takes you into Herring Run Park. Park at the end of this road and walk to Herring Run.

Rockhounding

The marble rocks are very hard, and when broken expose white crystalline marble.

Herring Run is a small stream that drains into Chesapeake Bay, and it is full of representative rocks from the various rock formations in the Piedmont. The section reached from the parking area is an interesting and easily accessible site on the eastern side of the city of Baltimore. It is a key city park and you can expect a lot of people in the parking lot and picnic areas, but I did not see many people in or along Herring Run.

The best time to visit the site is during low water, as during flooding the rocks may not be easy to see and access to Herring Run will be limited. The overall appearance of the streambed is white due to the high percentage of rounded rocks of Cockeysville marble. Many of these are nearly a foot long and almost entirely white. Orange feldspar from pegmatitic zones in the various gneissic rocks that eroded from the Piedmont can be found among the white marble rocks, and cracking these open often reveals large feldspar crystals with excellent reflective cleavage planes. A great deal of rounded conglomerate, which appears to be from the Loudoun Formation, is present, and some of this resembles rounded pieces of ready-mix concrete, which can also be found in the stream. During a visit in July 2014, I also found a large, rounded rock that was mostly calcite, and this had clear calcite in its interior. I kept looking for a long time for another large piece with similar clear calcite, but was only able to find large rocks of white marble and orange feldspar.

Unfortunately there is also a high percentage of plastic, glass, and other trash in the stream, and the City of Baltimore has posted signs stating the water is contaminated with sewage and that contact with the water should be avoided. Sewage runoff into city creeks is very common in older urban areas, and you must not make the mistake of taking a cooling dip in the clear waters of Herring Run on a hot day, as you might get extremely sick due to a terrible infection from any minor skin cut that comes in contact with the polluted water. This also goes for walking into the creek, especially if you do not have waterproof boots. I made it a point to stay out of the water and kept my feet and hands dry.

In addition to the alluvial rocks in Herring Run, there is a section of large slabs of Wissahickon schist on the west bank of the stream just north of the small bridge that crosses the creek from the parking area. From the opposite bank, these appear to be just tumbled blocks of boring schist, and they appear to have been placed as part of the construction along the stream. However, when you cross the bridge and climb onto these rocks, you can see that they are highly crenulated micaceous schists, and the mica gives them a very silvery appearance, especially in bright sunlight. The schists have minor zones of pegmatites, and these are full of orange feldspar, gray quartz, and stubby crystals of black tourmaline. The black tourmaline, which is also known as schorl, is easy to find and can be seen on many of the larger slabs of schists. The area has undoubtedly been well picked over by previous rockhounds, so I was surprised to see that so much tourmaline was still present.

The blocks of schists appear that they might be temporary and may be removed or covered during later construction, so it is uncertain if they will be here in the future. In the meantime, in the event you visit this site and come across new areas where bedrock has been excavated for sewers or bridges, any newly uncovered rocks will be well worth checking for tourmaline.

Reference: Cleaves, 1968

27. Herring Run River Rocks and Glass

This large bank has a virtually unlimited supply of rocks.

See map page 102.

County: Baltimore

Site type: Stream rocks

Land status: City of Baltimore park

Material: Ironstone, conglomerate, feldspar, marble, glass

Host rock: Various formations

Difficulty: Easy

Family-friendly: Yes

Tools needed: None, but a hammer is useful

Special concerns: May be inaccessible during high water

Special attractions: Baltimore Inner Harbor

GPS parking: 39°18'20"N / 76°32'43"W

GPS stream bank: 39°18'28"N / 76°32'38"W
Topographic quadrangle: Baltimore East, MD
Finding the site: From I-895, take exit 14 for Moravia Road East/Pulaski Highway. Take the ramp to US 40 West, also known as the Pulaski Highway, and go 0.8 mile, then turn right onto Armistead Way and go about 200 feet. Take the first right onto Alricks Way and look for a parking area just east of some residences. Park here and follow the trail to Herring Run. The area is very heavily overgrown and it may be difficult to see the large bank of rocks; you may have to follow one of the smaller overgrown trails to get to the rocks, which are on the west side of a very large elbow in the stream.

Rockhounding

This piece of hematitic-limonitic sandstone was found on the rocks next to the creek.

This site formed at a very large elbow in Herring Run, and it is easily visible on satellite photos of the area. The site features the various alluvial materials that wash down the stream. Herring Run drains sections of both the Baltimore Piedmont and the Atlantic Coastal Plain, and you can find pieces of gneiss, feldspar, marble, quartzite, conglomerate, and iron stone. The Piedmont rocks include rocks from the Baltimore gneiss, various schists, and Cockeysville marble, and the Atlantic Coastal Plain sediments include rocks from the Potomac Group, including rocks from the Arundel Clay and Patapsco Formation.

The stream-bank rocks are much smaller than the rocks found in the upstream areas of Herring Run Park. Most of the rocks found at this elbow are relatively small, and you can expect that the largest rocks you will find will be about 6 inches long, with most of them being just 1 to 2 inches in length and width. With a hammer you can break apart the rocks and see if you can find fresh cleavage surfaces on the feldspar and mineralized interiors within the iron stones. The conglomerate pieces are well-rounded and are also quite attractive, especially the rounded fist-size pieces.

Not surprisingly, since it drains an urban part of Baltimore, the bank is also loaded with polished glass. Some of the glass is still in shard form but there is a surprising amount of rounded glass, and it reminded me of many sea glass sites along the shores of Chesapeake Bay. There is also a fair amount of blue grass, as well as the standard white, green, and brown glass. On the hike to the site, I noticed a large amount of blue glass on the trail, which suggested that part of the area just east of the development and west of Herring Run may have been used for a dump in years past.

Reference: Cleaves et al., 1968.

28. Robert E. Lee Park Serpentine and Chromite

This small prospect pit is just north of the Yellow Trail.

See map page 102.

County: Baltimore
Site type: Trail outcrops and prospect pits
Land status: Baltimore County park
Material: Serpentine and chromite
Host rock: Ultramafic rocks
Difficulty: Easy
Family-friendly: Yes
Tools needed: None; collecting not allowed
Special concerns: Moderate hike to site, parking lot may be full during high season
Special attractions: Baltimore Inner Harbor

GPS parking: 39°22'45"N / 76°38'30"W
GPS chromite prospect: 39°23'11"N / 76°39'11"W
Topographic quadrangle: Cockeysville, MD
Finding the site: From I-83 North from Baltimore, take exit 10A for the Northern Parkway East. Merge onto the parkway and continue east for about 0.2 mile. Turn left (north) onto Falls Road and continue 0.9 mile. Look for the sign for Robert E. Lee Park and turn right (east) onto Lakeside Drive. Go about 0.6 mile, pass the dam, and park in the parking area. Look at the map posted at the parking area, then follow the paved loop to the Red Trail, which crosses an active rail line. Take the Red Trail to the Green Trail and go left (west), then continue to the intersection with the Yellow Trail and go left (south) on the Yellow Trail. The Yellow Trail crosses the main part of the serpentine rocks at the park, and a small chromite prospect pit is on the north side of the Yellow Trail near the western end of this trail.

Rockhounding

The chromite deposits in the ultramafic rocks of Robert E. Lee Park were part of the Bare Hills chromite district, which should not be confused with the Bare Hills copper mine. Robert E. Lee Park is a popular Baltimore County park, and the areas underlain by serpentine-derived soils are shown on the park map near the parking area.

This piece of chromite and serpentine was found on the ground surface near a small prospect pit.

The chromite deposits were worked in the early 1800s and have long been abandoned. The park also had a rail line. Some of the old rail tracks are still present along the Red Trail, but the trees that have grown between the tracks show how long it has been since trains have been on this trail. During my hike to the serpentine rock areas of the park, I met a man using a metal detector. He had a Baltimore County permit for metal detecting in county parks, and based on old maps he thought that he was at the site of a former train station along the long-abandoned railroad that crossed part of the park. The railroad bed was still present, and huge trees had grown between what used to be the railroad tracks. It looked like a great place to use a metal detector, but all he had found were iron spikes and coal slag, and his findings reminded me of why I largely have abandoned metal detecting in favor of looking at rocks.

Once you reach the Yellow Trail, you can see serpentine rock in outcrops on the trail. Most of the rock is weathered and greenish gray, and bands of fibrous blue-green serpentine can be seen on the trail. A chromite prospect pit is just off the Yellow Trail near its western end, and this has a small dump of weathered serpentine surrounding the opening. It is a very small prospect and is very easy to miss while hiking on the trail, but the GPS coordinates above should take you right to the prospect. I did not see any chromite on this dump, but in the woods on the south side of the trail opposite the pit are several dark, dense, heavy rocks that have black bands of chromite. There are almost certainly other small pits in the area, but these were the only prospects that I saw along the Yellow Trail.

References: Pearre and Heyl, 1960; Cleaves, 1968; Newcomb, 1994

29. Falls Road Serpentine Quarry

The Falls Road quarry is heavily overgrown, but the highwalls are still well exposed.

See map page 102.
County: Baltimore
Site type: Former quarry
Land status: Baltimore County park
Material: Serpentine
Host rock: Serpentine
Difficulty: Easy
Family-friendly: Yes
Tools needed: None; collecting not allowed
Special concerns: Area is overgrown during summer, ticks and mosquitoes
Special attractions: Baltimore Inner Harbor
GPS parking: 39°23'16"N / 76°39'34"W
GPS quarry: 39°23'13"N / 76°39'32"W

Topographic quadrangle: Cockeysville, MD

Finding the site: From I-83 North from Baltimore, take exit 10A for the Northern Parkway East. Merge onto the parkway and continue east for about 0.2 mile. Turn left (north) onto Falls Road and continue 2 miles. The parking area is approximately 100 feet north of the intersection of Falls Road and Coppermine Terrace. Park here, walk towards the stream, cross it, and then climb up the slope to the quarry.

Rockhounding

This is a large quarry that was excavated in the serpentine just east of Falls Road, and it is within the limits of Robert E. Lee Park. There is a similar quarry on private land just west of Falls Road along Coppermine Terrace. The quarry is very old and has not been worked for decades, as evidenced by the significant tree growth on the quarry floor and even the quarry highwalls.

The serpentine shows some good banding and variation in color.

The parking on Falls Road is adequate for a few cars, but finding the quarry can be tricky. The key to finding the quarry is to walk eastward, cross the stream, and then walk southeast. You will soon find a slope that looks man-made, as it is very long and flat on top. This is apparently the toe of the slope formed by the rocks that were pulled out of the quarry. It is a very short climb up this slope and then you should be able to see the quarry highwalls, which form a rough cliff. The trees are very thick, and even though the quarry is fairly large, it is easy to miss if you are not observant and looking for signs of a quarry.

The rocks on the highwalls and the floor of the quarry are almost entirely serpentine, and much of the rock is weathered and partially altered to chlorite and limonite. The quarry has some areas of slickensides and veins of fibrous serpentine minerals, but the vast bulk of the rock is massive, barren serpentine. I looked very hard for indications of chromite, copper, and other metallic minerals, but did not see any zones of metallic minerals. Based on the size of the quarry and the lack of significant chromite or copper mineralization, it appears that this quarry was used to supply aggregate for road construction and was not a metal mine. I did not see any indications of old crushing equipment or other heavy metal pieces, and since the material is already relatively soft and fractured, it may have been largely excavated with hand tools or other low-tech methods.

Reference: Eckert, 2000

30. Bare Hills Copper Mine Hornblende Schist–Chalcopyrite

This small creek drains the former area of the Bare Hills Copper Mine, and some mineralized amphiolites can be found in the drainage.

See map page 102.
County: Baltimore
Site type: Streambed
Land status: Private, but not posted
Material: Chalcopyrite
Host rock: Hornblende schist
Difficulty: Moderate to difficult
Family-friendly: No
Tools needed: Hammer
Special concerns: Limited parking, land status, garbage in creek
Special attractions: Baltimore Inner Harbor
GPS parking: 39°22'34"N / 76°39'36"W

GPS streambed: 39°22'30"N / 76°39'37"W
Topographic quadrangles: Cockeysville, MD, and Baltimore West, MD
Finding the site: From I-83 North from Baltimore, take exit 10A for Northern Parkway East. Go about 0.2 mile east and turn left (north) onto Falls Road. Continue 0.4 mile north on Falls Road and turn left (west) onto Kelly Avenue. Go 0.3 mile and turn right (north) onto Greely Road. Go about 400 feet and take the first left onto Smith Avenue. Go 0.7 mile, and Smith Avenue will begin a broad turn to the west. Right before this broad turn is Copper Ridge Drive, which leads to an apartment complex. I parked here in a spot next to plenty of open parking spaces, but bear in mind that this is a private complex and parking may be restricted. Alternatively you can park near the dumpsters next to Smith Avenue, but at the time of my visit, the dumpsters were overflowing and a steady stream of apartment dwellers continued to dump garbage into the bins, and I wanted to make sure that I was not blocking parking for any emergency trash pickup.

Rockhounding

The Bare Hills copper mine operated from the mid-1800s to about the beginning of the 1900s. It was a relatively small operation compared to some of the other copper deposits in Maryland, such as the Mineral Hill mine near Liberty Reservoir, and the mining was almost entirely underground by a shaft that was inclined to the southeast beneath Smith Avenue. The host rock of the copper minerals was mainly hornblende schist.

Virtually all traces of the mine and mine dumps have been obliterated by the apartment complex and surrounding development. However, if you walk south of the stormwater collection pond on the north side of Smith Avenue and look at the barren areas on the hill slope, you can see old bricks, ceramics, and other indications of the former mining complex. Since the area had extensive mine dumps, it seemed reasonable that some of the mined rocks would be present in the stream along Smith Avenue. However, when I walked along the stream north of Copper Ridge Drive, I did not see any malachite staining or other indications of copper mineralization. I later walked farther downstream and hiked into the stream just south of Copper Ridge Drive. This area is just adjacent to Smith Avenue and is not posted against trespassing. I found a very tiny piece of malachite and noticed that many of the rocks in the stream were large pieces of hornblende schist.

Most of these were barren of mineralization, but I found some that had reddish staining, and on breaking them open found that some had metallic mineralization. The area in the stream is very dark, as the tree cover is extensive, but when I brought the pieces into the light, I could see that they had grains of chalcopyrite and some iridescent metallic grains that resembled bornite. Bornite is also known as "peacock ore," as this iridescence is much like the colors of a peacock. In my experience, bornite is relatively uncommon, and it is easy to confuse with discolored chalcopyrite. However, bornite has been reported from this locality, so it is possible that the iridescent minerals are bornite. Chalcopyrite and bornite are considered primary minerals, as they represent the first copper minerals formed, as opposed to secondary minerals such as malachite and azurite that form when a deposit is oxidized or otherwise altered. Some of the hornblende crystals were also fairly coarse, which was a bonus that I did not expect.

This rock has abundant chalcopyrite in a hornblende-rich rock, and may represent typical ores from this former copper mine.

I was very surprised that only a tiny amount of malachite was present in this drainage, and I did not see any indications of azurite, which would be easy to spot since it is typically bright blue. Normally the drainages next to abandoned copper mines have an abundance of malachite and some very minor azurite, as the copper ores near the surface are often oxidized. In this case the copper minerals, which were mined at depth, may have remained unoxidized and the primary sulfide minerals stayed largely intact. Alternatively collectors may have also removed all of the malachite over the years. It was actually interesting to find a copper mine that had primary sulfides such as chalcopyrite and bornite as the dominant copper-bearing minerals. The hornblende schist with the sulfides can make good display pieces, but some are so large that they will take up a lot of space in your collection.

You must be aware that this is a very filthy stream and take the appropriate precautions if you enter this drainage. It has a lot of litter, and the overflowing dumpsters next to the apartment complex undoubtedly get flooded by stormwater and drain right into the creek. The bacteria levels must be extremely high in this drainage. Make sure you have suitable footwear, long pants, and gloves if you climb into this creek to look for mineralized rocks.

Reference: Moore, 1994

31. Gunpowder River Garnet and Crenulated Schist

Garnets can be easily seen on the weathered surfaces of loose rocks around the outcrops.

County: Baltimore
Site type: Outcrops and loose rocks along river near bridge
Land status: Loch Raven Reservoir property
Material: Garnet and crenulated schists
Host rock: Loch Raven schist
Difficulty: Easy
Family-friendly: Yes
Tools needed: None; collecting not allowed
Special concerns: Limited parking, slopes can be steep
Special attractions: Fishing in Loch Raven Reservoir
GPS parking: 39°30'05"N / 76°37'27"W
GPS outcrops: 39°30'05"N / 76°37'27"W

Topographic quadrangle: Phoenix, MD

Finding the site: From I-83 North from Baltimore, take I-695 East for 1.5 miles, then stay right to exit onto I-83 North towards York, Pennsylvania. Take exit 18 to merge onto West Warren Road toward Cockeysville. Go 1.4 miles and turn left onto York Road. Go 1.2 miles and turn right onto MD 145 East. Continue on MD 145 East for 1.6 miles, and you will approach a bridge that crosses Loch Raven Reservoir. Park on the north side of the road, just west of the bridge, and make sure that you are well off the road. There is also parking on the east side, but it is limited to only one or two vehicles. From here hike to the slopes on the side of the reservoir to find the garnets and crenulated schist.

Rockhounding

This is an outstanding location with large garnets and crenulated schists of the Loch Raven schist. The Loch Raven schist is late Precambrian/early Paleozoic and formed from the metamorphism of coarse sandstones and clays. The access areas are mainly used for fishing, but they offer an excellent opportunity to visit these rock outcrops.

This site is next to a former bridge, which is closed and posted against trespassing. I was able to walk around the bridge down towards the reservoir without encountering any signs indicating that access to the lake is prohibited. I was at the site in early spring and still encountered a fair amount of brush, and the slopes were fairly steep. I did not have to go all the way to the lake, and I stayed focused on the large outcrops on the upper side of the west bank. I soon came to very large exposures of silvery schists with garnets.

Both loose rocks and rocks in outcrop can be observed. The garnets are principally almandine, and I saw garnets up to a quarter inch in diameter. Staurolite and kyanite are also reported to be in the Loch Raven schist in this region, but I did not see any during my visit. The

This crenulated schist shows excellent chevron folds and is a great teaching aid as well as a great display piece.

schist has some very distinct folds which are excellent examples of deformation in metamorphic rocks. Some of the best garnets are exposed on weathered surfaces, while some of the best folded schists are observed by breaking off unweathered sections of rock and looking at the crenulations. The crenulations are textbook examples of folds and deformation during metamorphism, and the garnets are also good examples of porphyroblasts in schist.

Reference: Cleaves, 1968

Sites 31–34

83
45
Loch Raven Reservoir
145
31
32
33
Paper Mill Rd.
Western Run
Shawan Rd.
Hunt Valley
Shawan Rd.
34
Oregon Pool
Oregon Branch
McCormick Rd.
45
OREGON RIDGE PARK
Beaver Dam Rd.
Cockeysville
York Rd.
Beaverdam Pond
83
N
0 0.5 mi.
0 0.5 km.

32. Hunt Valley McCormick Road Marble

The marble outcrops are a prominent feature of the east end of McCormick Road.

See map page 121.
County: Baltimore
Site type: Outcrops along road
Land status: Private, but not posted
Material: Marble
Host rock: Cockeysville marble
Difficulty: Easy
Family-friendly: Yes
Tools needed: None; hammering at site not recommended.
Special concerns: Land status uncertain
Special attractions: Hunt Valley Town Centre
GPS parking: 39°30'03"N / 76°39'05"W

The marble is very white and shows some banding when observed at the outcrops.

Topographic quadrangle: Hereford, MD

Finding the site: From I-83, take exit 20A for Shawan Road East. Go approximately 0.5 mile, then turn left onto McCormick Road and continue 0.7 mile. You will see the outcrops on your left (north). A road to the left (north), which has a closed gate up the hill, offers an area for parking. Walk to the outcrops from here.

Rockhounding

This is one of the best exposures of Cockeysville marble in Maryland. Cockeysville marble is a late Precambrian white crystalline metamorphosed limestone. The marble was used for the construction of the Washington Monument. The first 152 feet of the monument came from a quarry in the Cockeysville marble just south of Hunt Valley in Texas, Maryland, between 1845 and 1854. Funds were depleted and the Civil War started, and construction did not begin again until 1879, but then it was built with a stone from Massachusetts. This proved to be too costly, and the monument was finally finished with marble from a quarry near Cockeysville, Maryland. Cockeysville marble was used for many other buildings in Baltimore and Washington, DC.

Today the marble is mined to produce crushed stone for aggregate, and it has also been processed into high-purity calcium carbonate for use in the paint, agriculture, and building industries.

The outcrops are adjacent to McCormick Road and relatively easy to reach. The slopes adjacent to the outcrops are heavily overgrown with grass and briars during the summer but are relatively clear in early spring. There is not a lot of talus below the outcrops, and the marble is still very solid. The rocks show strong banding, and the dip of the marble beds is readily apparent. These are outcrops that are best left preserved, and you should leave your hammer in the car when you visit this site.

References: Purdum, 1940; Cleaves, 1968; Kuff and Brooks, 1990

33. Hunt Valley Mall Garnet

The site is on a hillside just north of the Hunt Valley mall.

See map page 121.
County: Baltimore
Site type: Outcrops on hillside
Land status: Private, but not posted
Material: Garnet and micaceous schist
Host rock: Late Precambrian Setters Formation schist
Difficulty: Easy
Family-friendly: Yes
Tools needed: None; hammering not recommended
Special concerns: Land status, right next to mall
Special attractions: Hunt Valley Towne Centre
GPS parking: 39°29'58"N / 76°39'27"W
Topographic quadrangle: Cockeysville, MD

Finding the site: From I-83, take exit 20A for Shawan Road East. Go approximately 0.5 mile and turn left onto McCormick Road. Continue 0.1 mile and turn right onto International Circle, then turn left. Follow the road along the parking lot for about 0.2 mile and park next to the schist outcrops on the side of the hill, which is north of the parking lot.

Rockhounding

This is a well-known outcrop of garnet-rich micaceous schist. It is exposed on the hillside north of Hunt Valley Towne Centre, which is also known simply as the Hunt Valley mall. The garnets are within a pelitic schist section of the Setters Formation, which is late Precambrian.

This is a classic suburban site, as you can park your car and walk about 30 feet on asphalt pavement to the outcrop. There are very few places that are so accessible. However, it is another example of an outcrop that is best left preserved from hammering. Many rockhounds, especially geology students from universities, have taken field trips to this site. Fortunately natural erosion provides a fair amount of loose rocks at the base of the hillside. In addition to the prominent garnets, you can see staurolite crystals on the surface of the schists. Kyanite is also reported to occur on this hillside, but I did not see any kyanite during my visit to the site.

References: Crowley et al., 1976; Lang, 1996

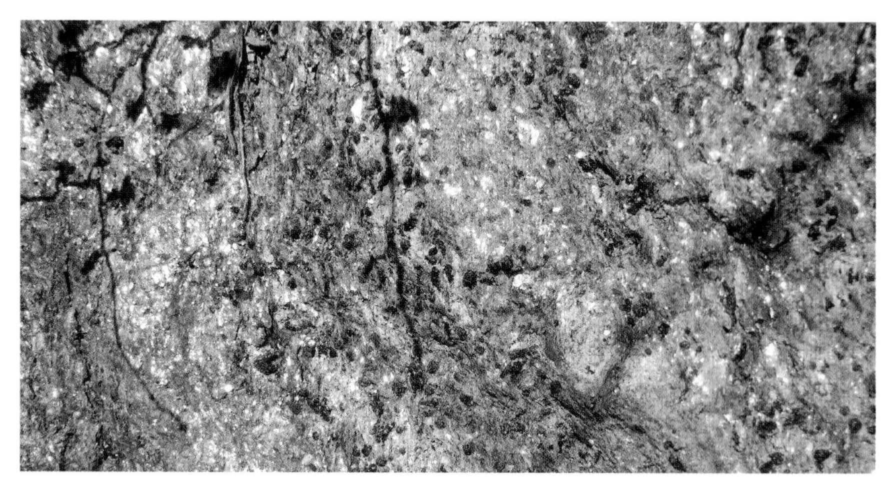

The garnets are very easy to see in this part of the Loch Raven schist.

34. Oregon Ridge Goethite and Marble

The former iron mine west of the nature center has steep sides, and the former mine floor is sometimes flooded.

See map page 121.

County: Baltimore
Site type: Former iron pit and small marble quarry
Land status: Baltimore County Department of Recreation and Parks
Material: Goethite and marble
Host rock: Loch Raven schist and Cockeysville marble
Difficulty: Easy to moderate
Family-friendly: Yes
Tools needed: None
Special concerns: No collecting allowed
Special attractions: Oregon Ridge Nature Center, swimming pond, hiking trails
GPS parking: 39°29'38"N / 76°41'23"W
GPS iron ore pit: 39°29'39"N / 76°41'35"W
GPS marble quarry: 39°29'42"N / 76°41'32"W
Topographic quadrangle: Cockeysville, MD

Finding the site: From I-83, take exit 20B to Shawan Road and go west for about 1.2 miles. Turn left onto Beaver Dam Road and take the first right onto Kurtz Lane. Go about 0.4 mile and park here. The former iron and marble mines are just west of the park nature center building along well-defined trails.

Rockhounding

This site has a small former iron mine, a former marble quarry, and a former iron mine that is now a lake, as well as an old iron furnace. The mines and furnace operated from 1844 to 1858. The area has been owned by the Baltimore County Department of Recreation and Parks since 1969, and it is a very popular park for locals.

This piece of goethite was observed on the west side of the former iron mine.

Oregon Ridge is a very big park, and when I first visited it, I was uncertain about the location of the iron mines. At first I hiked south on the trails that led from the main parking area. Some of the rocks on the hillsides had large exposures of silvery garnetiferous Loch Raven schist, but no iron ore. I later found out that the area on the west side of the park is the site of a former iron mine and marble quarry, and I could have saved myself some considerable time and hiking if I had known this from the start. Interestingly, even though there was a very large goethite rock in the woods near the iron mine display, the mine area itself is relatively barren of goethite. I found some interesting pieces of goethite under some leaves on the hillside of the former iron mine, but not as much as I would have expected for this type of open-pit mine. The marble quarry was also surprisingly bare of exposed marble. It was heavily overgrown with vegetation, and difficult to walk down to the floor of the quarry.

The park has done an excellent job with the iron ore and marble quarry displays. The swimming lake is also a former iron mine that has long been filled with water, and goethite-bearing rocks can be found on the steep hillsides of the lake. The former furnace is located just west of the park entrance road, and pieces of slag can still be found around the furnace. Unfortunately rock collecting is not allowed in the park.

References: Cleaves et al., 1968; Crowley et al., 1976; Mackay, 1995

35. Soldiers Delight Serpentine

The serpentine is well exposed on the trails in the Soldiers Delight NEA.

County: Baltimore
Site type: Serpentine and former chromite mines
Land status: Maryland Department of Natural Resources Natural Environment Area
Material: Serpentine and chromite
Host rock: Serpentine
Difficulty: Easy to moderate
Family-friendly: Yes
Tools needed: None
Special concerns: Maryland DNR land; no collecting allowed
Special attractions: Soldiers Delight Visitor Center
GPS parking: 39°24'52"N / 76°50'09"W
GPS Choate Mine: 39°24'46"N / 76°50'03"W

GPS pit mine: 39°24'59"N / 77°49'53"W
Topographic quadrangle: Reisterstown, MD
Finding the site: Take I-695 to exit 19 and head north on I-795. Go 6.7 miles and take exit 7B for Franklin Boulevard West. Continue 0.5 mile, take a slight right onto Church Road, and go 0.8 mile to Berrymans Lane. Turn left (south) and go 0.4 mile, then take the first left (south) onto Deer Park Road and continue 1 mile. The parking area will be to your right (west). Park here and cross the road to the trails on the east side of the road to the Soldiers Delight Natural Environment Area.

Rockhounding

Soldiers Delight is a Natural Environment Area (NEA) that covers about 1,900 acres (approximately 3 square miles) in western Baltimore County. The area is almost entirely underlain by serpentine bedrock. Serpentine is formed from metamorphism of mafic rocks that are high in iron and magnesium and low in silica and aluminum. The high iron and magnesium content turns the soils orange to red, and plants generally find it difficult to grow in the soil. This leads to the description of the area as a "serpentine barrens."

This is an example of some of the blue-green serpentine visible near the Pit Mine.

The area east of the parking lot has a trail that leads to the Choate Mine and the Pit Mine. The trail is a circular loop, and you can reach both mines very easily. I started on the south end of the trail and quickly arrived at the Choate Mine. The mine openings were full of water and surrounded by a fence, and there were not any significant mining dumps around the mine. As I continued eastward, serpentine bedrock was exposed along much of the trail. At the time of my visit in early May 2014, the trail was very wet and it was hard to keep my feet dry.

The trail soon turns northward, and you can follow this north until it turns west. You will soon arrive at the Pit Mine, which consists of some small pits on the north side of the trail. I found the serpentine on the trail near the Pit Mine to be much more colorful than the serpentine near the Choate Mine. Many pieces of serpentine appeared polished and waxy, and some had fibrous green sections. The colors ranged from very light green to green to light blue. I also found a very dense rock near the opening of the small, fenced, shaft Pit Mine. I interpreted this piece to be serpentine with chromite and magnetite, as it had very small, distinct black grains. Unfortunately, since this is an NEA, collecting is not allowed, but at least it is possible to visit these mines and see the excellent exposures of serpentine in this serpentine barren.

References: Pearre and Heyl, 1960; Bernstein, 1980

Sites 35–42

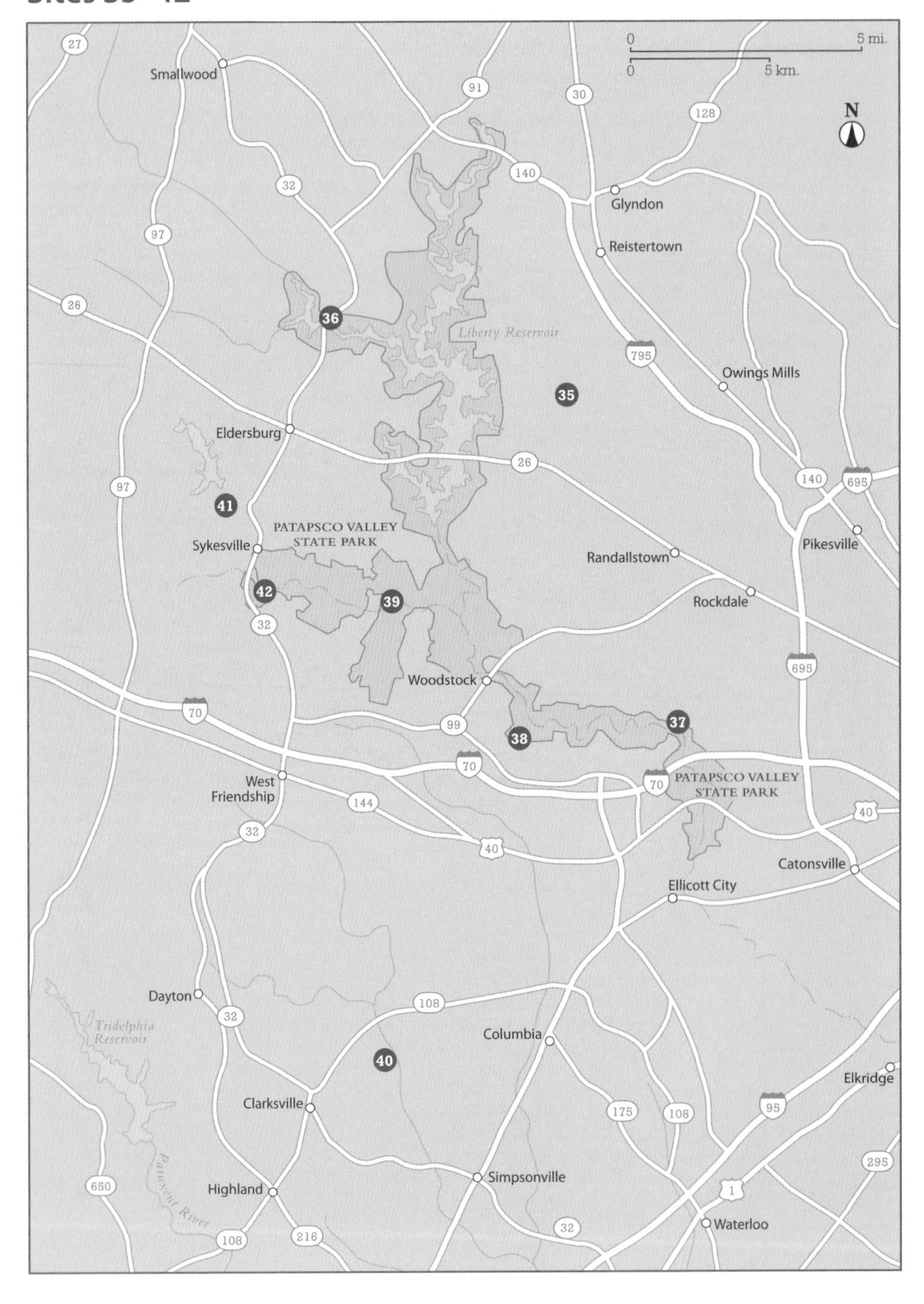

0
5 mi.
0
5 km.
N
Smallwood
Glyndon
Reistertown
Liberty Reservoir
Owings Mills
Eldersburg
Randallstown
Pikesville
PATAPSCO VALLEY STATE PARK
Sykesville
Rockdale
Woodstock
West Friendship
PATAPSCO VALLEY STATE PARK
Catonsville
Ellicott City
Dayton
Tridelphia Reservoir
Columbia
Elkridge
Clarksville
Patuxent River
Simpsonville
Highland
Waterloo
35
36
37
38
39
40
41
42
27
91
30
128
140
32
97
26
795
695
99
70
144
40
108
175
95
295
1
650
216

36. Mineral Hill Mine Malachite and Talc Schist

The pit area is well exposed and has abundant malachite, talc schist, and actinolite.

See map page 132.
County: Carroll
Site type: Former mine dumps
Land status: Baltimore Department of Public Works
Material: Malachite, actinolite, talc
Host rock: Chlorite schists and fine-grained gneisses
Difficulty: Easy
Family-friendly: Yes
Tools needed: Hammer
Special concerns: Dump next to lake is very steep, pit area gets very hot in summer
Special attractions: Fishing in Liberty Reservoir

GPS parking: 39°26'18"N / 76°56'15"W
GPS lakeside mine dump: 39°26'13"N / 76°55'53"W
GPS pit: 39°26'18"N / 76°55'50"W
Topographic quadrangle: Finksburg, MD
Finding the site: From I-70, take exit 80 and head north on MD 32/Sykesville Road. Continue about 10 miles, and you will then begin to cross Liberty Reservoir. Cross the reservoir and park in the parking area on the east side of MD 32. From here follow the trails in the woods to the mine pit. The mine dump, while visible from the bridge, is not visible from the trail, but it is south of the former mine pit and on the north side of the reservoir.

Rockhounding

The Mineral Hill mine is a former copper mine that still has many collectible minerals. It is located adjacent to Liberty Reservoir and has public access. Liberty Reservoir is the public water supply for the city of Baltimore, and the Department of Public Works allows limited recreational use of the lake and adjacent lands. You will often see numerous cars at the public access areas and come across hikers on the trails and fishermen on the banks of the lake.

This talc schist was found on the dumps next to Liberty Reservoir.

The Mineral Hill mine is one of the oldest copper mines in Maryland. The mine was part of the Sykesville copper district and was mined before the Revolutionary War. It was opened by British interests soon after 1748. The size of the pre-Revolutionary workings indicate that a considerable amount of copper ore was removed between 1749 and 1776, but with the outbreak of the war, the mine closed. The owners moved back to England, and the mine was confiscated. It was not until 1849 that mining was restarted. It operated continuously from 1849 to 1890, with the greatest production prior to 1864. The host rock of the deposit is a dark green to light green schist, which ranges from chlorite schist to chlorite-amphibole or chlorite-talc schist. Serpentine is also present, as well as quartz-biotite schist, and some of the rocks are very coarse-grained and best described as gneissic.

The mine dump, which is right next to the lake, has abundant malachite and talc schists, and I have also found some asbestos-like minerals on this dump. The dump is very steep, and you have to be very careful when making your way down to the lake. The rocks are well exposed on the dump, and it is very easy to get distracted by the minerals that you can see as you climb downslope. I have also found that there is a lot of animal waste adjacent to the reservoir on the dump. Since Liberty Reservoir is used by Baltimore for its water supply, if there is an E. coli outbreak in the city and they cannot trace the source, here is a good place to look.

If you continue farther on the trail, you will soon come to a broad open pit. The minerals are different from those of the dump, as there are not as many copper minerals. However, there are many excellent pieces of talc and actinolite-rich schists. During the summer this area gets extremely hot, as the broad open pit is positioned to receive the maximum amount of sun during the day. Make sure you bring a hat—it does not take long to become overheated. Fortunately I had brought some water, and this is really important to bring if you are here in the summer.

References: Beard, 2008; Heyl and Pearre, 1965

37. Dogwood Creek Feldspar and Mica Schist

Dogwood Creek has abundant rocks of nearly all types.

See map page 132.

County: Baltimore

Site type: Rocks in streambed

Land status: Patapsco Valley State Park and unposted streambed

Material: Orange feldspar and coarse muscovite schist

Host rock: Pegmatitic gneiss and schist

Difficulty: Easy

Family-friendly: Yes

Tools needed: Hammer

Special concerns: Security at parking area

Special attractions: Patapsco Valley State Park

GPS parking: 39°18'56"N / 76°47'36"W

GPS streambed: 39°18'58"N / 76°47'36"W

Topographic quadrangle: Ellicott City, MD

Finding the site: From I-70, take exit 87 to US 29 North and turn right (east) onto Rogers Avenue. Continue about 0.7 mile to a traffic circle and take the third exit onto Old Frederick Road. Go about 1.7 miles, and this turns into Hollofield Road. Continue 0.3 mile north and turn left onto Dogwood Road. Cross Dogwood Creek and park in the parking area for Patapsco Valley State Park. A section of the streambed that is full of feldspar and mica schist is just north of the bridge.

Rockhounding

This is an example of graphic granite.

This is an interesting site that I found while looking for ultramafic and asbestos-bearing rocks that had eroded from the area of the Bok asbestos mine. The Bok asbestos mine is on private land in an area of partially amphibolized layered gabbro and pyroxenite, and it is upstream from this section of Dogwood Creek. Looking downgradient of private mines and outcrops is often a way to find rocks that cannot be accessed otherwise.

I visited Dogwood Creek in early August 2014 when the water level was low, and found an abundance of rocks exposed in the streambed just north of the bridge that crosses the creek. I was initially disappointed when I could not find any asbestos minerals, but I soon noticed that there were many large pieces of orange feldspar and very coarse muscovite schist. Breaking open these pieces revealed sections of feldspar with excellent cleavage, graphic granite patterns, and layers of coarse muscovite.

This was in an area just north of the state park land, and there were no indications that the streambed was posted, but the banks adjacent to the stream are obviously private land and should not be accessed. This site is also best observed when the water is low. During high water it obviously gets very rough, based on the large trees and other debris in the creek. This is also another good example of why you should always keep your eyes open for other rocks that may be of interest. I did not expect to find the feldspar and mica in this creek, but I considered these rocks to be among the best pieces that I have found in the Maryland Piedmont.

To access this site, I parked at the state park parking area just south of the bridge and on the west side of the creek. There were a few other cars parked in this area, and it was safe from the traffic, but there was a warning sign indicating that vehicles were commonly broken into at this parking area. If you park in this area, I would be very careful to not leave any valuables in your car, especially in areas where passersby can see them, and I would also minimize my time at this site and keep an eye on my car if at all possible.

References: Bernstein, 1980; Cleaves et al., 1968; Crowley, 1976

38. Frost Quarry Albite Feldspar

The former quarry dumps are easy to see in the woods, and the sides are loaded with large pieces of pegmatitic albite feldspar and quartz.

See map page 132.
County: Howard
Site type: Former quarry
Land status: Patapsco Valley State Park
Material: Albite feldspar and quartz
Host rock: Pegmatite intruding Woodstock gneiss and Cockeysville marble
Difficulty: Easy
Family-friendly: Yes
Tools needed: None; collecting not allowed
Special concerns: Snakes, poison ivy
Special attractions: Patapsco Valley State Park
GPS parking: 39°18'48"N / 76°51'24"W
GPS quarry: 39°18'48"N / 76°25'31"W
Topographic quadrangle: Ellicott City, MD

Finding the site: From I-70 West, merge onto US 29 North, which ends almost immediately, and turn left onto MD 99, which is also Old Frederick Road. Go 2.9 miles and turn right (northeast) onto Green Clover Drive. Continue 0.8 mile and look for a small gate to a service road into the woods. This leads into Patapsco Valley State Park. You can park on the small shoulder near the gate. Walk down the road and head upstream up the small gully to your left. You will be walking almost due west. Follow the faint trails to the former Frost feldspar quarry.

Rockhounding

This is an excellent site for feldspar, and is an easy-to-reach location that just requires a slight hike through the woods. Assuming you approach the quarry area from the east, you will see numerous pieces of albite feldspar and dark gray quartz. The intergrowths of feldspar and quartz make an interesting pattern on the rock. The dumps are very extensive and are loaded with large pieces of feldspar.

This is a typical piece of albite feldspar-quartz pegmatite at the former Frost quarry.

The quarry was operated in the early part of the 1900s for feldspar. The main workings are flooded, and the area is overgrown with trees. However, the extent of the dumps is easy to establish. While the tops of the dumps are flat and covered with grass, the sides are exposed and have an abundance of large rocks that are mostly white feldspar. Most of the rocks that I saw were feldspar and quartz, but beryl, diopside, and titanite are also reported to occur at this site.

References: Ostrander and Price, 1940; Bernstein, 1980

39. Henryton Tunnel Area Feldspar Quarry

The quarry highwall is approximately 50 to 60 feet high, but it is hard to see until you climb up the north bank of the river.

See map page 132.
County: Carroll
Site type: Former quarry
Land status: Patapsco Valley State Park
Material: Albite feldspar and muscovite
Host rock: Lower pelitic schist of the Glenarm series
Difficulty: Easy
Family-friendly: No; have to cross river
Tools needed: None
Special concerns: State park; no collecting allowed
Special attractions: Fishing in the Patapsco River
GPS parking: 39°21'06"N / 76°53'56"W
GPS quarry: 39°21'13"N / 76°54'29"W

Topographic quadrangle: Sykesville, MD

Finding the site: From I-70 West, take exit 83 for Marriottsville Road. Continue 3.4 miles north and park in the parking area on the left (west) side of Marriottsville Road next to the railroad tracks. From here hike approximately 0.75 mile to the bridge that crosses the Patapsco River, which is just before the Henryton Tunnel. This is your key landmark to get oriented. From the bridge, look for small trails in the woods that go downstream, and from the south bank of the river, look for a broad flat area on the north side of the river. This is the floor of the quarry. The quarry is on the north side of the river, approximately 500 feet downstream from the bridge.

Rockhounding

Pegamtitic zones along the quarry highwalls have quartz, white albite feldspar, and silvery muscovite.

This site is a former feldspar mine that operated on the north bank of the Patapsco River. The Henryton Tunnel is a useful way to help you find the quarry, as the quarry is just downstream of the tunnel. The Henryton Tunnel is reportedly the third-oldest tunnel in the world that is in use, and trains pass through it frequently. The tunnel was constructed by the Baltimore & Ohio Railroad and opened around 1850, and was rebuilt to its current form in 1903. The tunnel was also used as a way to get to the former Henryton State Hospital, which was a hospital complex that closed in 1985 and was finally demolished in 2013. The complex was said to be haunted, but in reality the biggest threats were asbestos, mold, structural collapse, and getting arrested for trespassing. Fortunately the feldspar quarry is far from the former hospital and on Patapsco Valley State Park land, so trespassing is not an issue at this site.

Train tunnels often have some interesting rocks near their openings, but the Henryton Tunnel just has gneiss, and I did not find any interesting rocks near the tunnel. For the purposes of this trip, however, it proves to be a useful landmark. At the time of our visit in August 2014, it was pouring rain, and it was shaping up to be an unsuccessful trip. We followed some of the trails that led to the Patapsco River, and were able to take some shelter under the trees. I had hoped to find some good pegmatitic rocks in the river, and noticed that the north bank had some very large boulders that appeared to not be natural. They looked like they had been excavated and rolled off the hillside. I looked upwards towards their source and saw a flat area that resembled a road, or perhaps the floor of a quarry, and we decided to cross the river to investigate. Fortunately, despite the rain, the river was still very low, and we were able to find a place that we could walk across. By this time we were quite soaked by the rain, and we had to fight the briars and slippery rocks to climb up the north bank.

We then saw the quarry face, which is quite large. The highwall is approximately 50 to 60 feet high and is feldspar-rich gneiss with pegmatitic zones of coarse white feldspar and books of muscovite. The rocks are very solid, and large mica books protrude from the quarry highwalls. The feldspar appears to be albite, based on the white color. The area does not appear to get many visitors, as the quarry floor was heavily overgrown with vegetation. This quarry is also reportedly one of three quarries known as the Devries Quarries, but we only found one quarry in the area. Our visit was cut short by the rain, and the vegetation made it difficult to move farther upstream or downstream.

Reference: Cleaves et al., 1968

40. Middle Patuxent Banded Marble and Graphic Granite

This is a good example of the graphic granite found at this site.

See map page 132.
County: Howard
Site type: Streambeds and ground surface
Land status: Middle Patuxent Environmental Area
Material: Banded marble and graphic granite
Host rock: None; loose rocks in tributaries and river
Difficulty: Easy
Family-friendly: Yes
Tools needed: None; collecting not allowed
Special concerns: Some areas inaccessible during high water
Special attractions: Patuxent River State Park
GPS parking: 39°12'45"N / 76°55'07"W
GPS bridge over tributary: 39°13'02"N / 76°54'33"W
GPS gravel bank on river: 39°13'06"N / 76°54'37"W

Topographic quadrangle: Clarksville, MD

Finding the site: From I-95, take exit 38B and merge onto MD 32 West. Go 5.5 miles and take the exit for Great Star Drive. Turn right onto Great Star Drive and take the first right onto Summer Sunrise Drive. Go about 500 feet and turn left onto Trotter Road. Go 1 mile and at the traffic circle continue straight on Trotter Road. Go 0.2 mile to the parking area on your right. From here follow the trails to the bridge above the tributary and to the gravel bank on the Middle Patuxent River. A GPS is highly recommended for this area.

Rockhounding

The Middle Patuxent Environmental Area (MPEA) is managed by the Howard County Department of Recreation and Parks in cooperation with the Middle Patuxent Environmental Foundation. The area covers over 1,000 acres and offers a welcome respite from the development between Baltimore and Washington, DC.

The banding in this marble is reportedly from layers of phlogopite, which are more resistant to weathering than the white marble.

Bedrock of the area is mapped as Baltimore gneiss and lower pelitic schist, and a band of Cockeysville marble is just northwest of the area. Bedrock, however, is almost entirely covered, and the most interesting rocks of the MPEA are found in the tributaries that drain into the Middle Patuxent River and in the gravel banks along the river. Some of the strangest-appearing rocks that I have found are the large pieces of white marble with prominent black bands of dark mica that I assume is biotite or phlogopite. The dark mica is resistant to weathering, and the marble is much softer and weathers away much quicker. These rocks are best found in the tributaries, especially in the areas near the wooden bridge that cross these small drainages. Large pieces of orange feldspar are common, and when broken they exhibit excellent cleavage and graphic granite patterns of intergrown quartz and feldspar. Unfortunately, as this is an environmental area, collecting of these rocks is not allowed.

Reference: Cleaves, 1968

41. Sykesville Mine Specular Hematite

The rocky area is a clearing just east of the main shaft.

See map page 132.
County: Carroll
Site type: Former iron mine
Land status: Nature preserve of Fairhaven Retirement Community
Material: Specular hematite
Host rock: Metavolcanic schist and gneiss of the Sykesville Formation
Difficulty: Easy
Family-friendly: Yes
Tools needed: None
Special concerns: Collecting likely not allowed
Special attractions: Patapsco Valley State Park
GPS parking: 39°22'44"N / 76°58'29"W
GPS rocky area: 39°22'54"N / 76°58'28"W

GPS large dump: 39°22'52"N / 76°58'30"W
Topographic quadrangle: Finksburg, MD
Finding the site: From I-70, take exit 80 to MD 32/Sykesville Road. Continue 3.9 miles and turn left (west) onto MD 851 North. Go 0.7 mile, and this turns into Spout Hill Road. Continue onto Spout Hill Road for 0.5 mile. Turn left onto Obrecht Road, go 0.2 mile, and turn right into the Copper Ridge Complex, which is right next to Fairhaven. The directions from here are somewhat tricky, as some streets names are not available via Google Maps. After you enter the complex, take the first right, go about 0.15 mile, and turn left, followed by a sharp left. Follow this road to the northwest until it ends near a gravel road. There are two visitor parking spaces here. From here follow the trails to the mine area. A GPS with the mine-area locations preloaded is highly recommended if you do not have a trail map.

Rockhounding

The Sykesville mine is sometimes referred to as the Springfield Mine or Mr. Tyson's Mine, and was opened in 1849 by Issac Tyson Jr. as an iron mine. It was briefly reopened around 1880 for iron, and was again operated briefly in 1916 by the Shawinigan Electro-Products Company for iron and quartz for the production of ferrosilicon. The mine is similar to the nearby Mineral Hill mine, but the Sykesville mine has a greater percentage of specular hematite and less magnetite than at Mineral Hill. The Sykesville mine was the chief source of iron for the Elba Furnace, which is located on the north side of the Patapsco River about 0.75 mile southeast of the mine. Copper was later discovered at depth, and the mine became a copper mine.

Specular hematite can be found in the rocky area and is very dense when compared to the non-mineralized schist.

The mine site is part of a nature trail at the Fairhaven Retirement Community. The nature trail is apparently open to the public, as it is not posted against trespassing, and I encountered some other hikers while on the trail. I used a map that was in a mailbox on the trail at "Shadyside Loop," which is on the southeast corner of the nature preserve. The map showed that the "Springfield Copper Mine" is on the west side of the preserve.

The mine area is in the woods and is located just off the trail. Some of the foundations for the main shaft area are located just east of a large mine dump, which is heavily overgrown with trees and briars. Immediately east of the concrete foundations is a rocky area that is in a small clearing. This area has very few trees or briars, and the lack of plants may be related to the high metal content of the rocks in this clearing. Many of the rocks are full of fine-grained specular hematite, and they are extremely dense when compared to non-mineralized rocks. Although previous descriptions of this site indicated that malachite is abundant, I only saw a small amount of this mineral. If I had not known about the copper mining, I would have been certain that this was simply an old iron mine. The specular hematite is easy to find and is often found as bands within the gneissic schists. Although there are no signs prohibiting collecting, I assume that since this is a nature preserve, collecting is not allowed.

References: Heyl and Pearre, 1965; Bernstein, 1980

42. Elba Furnace Glassy Slag

Some of the slag is both glassy and frothy.

See map page 132.
County: Carroll
Site type: Streambed
Land status: Patapsco Valley State Park
Material: Glassy slag
Host rock: Streambed
Difficulty: Easy
Family-friendly: Yes
Tools needed: None
Special concerns: State park; no collecting allowed
Special attractions: Fishing along South Branch of Patapsco River
GPS parking: 39°21'24"N / 76°57'32"W
GPS furnace: 39°21'25"N / 76°57'35"W
GPS stream gravels with glassy slag: 39°21'26"N / 76°57'31"W
Topographic quadrangle: Sykesville, MD
Finding the site: From I-70, take exit 80 to merge onto MD 32 North/Sykesville Road. Go about 3.9 miles and turn left onto MD 851 North. Go 0.3 mile and take

This piece of slag resembles broken obsidian with a pronounced conchoidal fracture.

a right (east) onto River Road. Follow this to the GPS coordinates for the parking. Walk across the South Branch of the Patapsco River, and you will be able to see the remains of the furnace in the woods. The glassy slag can be found in the large gravel banks just downstream of the furnace.

Rockhounding

The Elba Furnace, built in 1847, was a steam and charcoal furnace that was about 30 feet high with an inside diameter of 8.5 feet wide. The furnace roasted iron ore from the Springfield mine. It was considered to be an efficient blast furnace and in 1857 was rated at 1,500 tons per year. However, a major flood in 1868 that destroyed much of Sykesville also heavily damaged the furnace, and it was never rebuilt. The area around the furnace was reported to be scattered with slag.

This furnace caught my attention, as some of the older iron furnaces often have abundant glassy slag. The remains of the furnace are still standing on the north bank of the Patapsco River and they are easy to find, provided you have either a topographic map or the proper GPS coordinates. Otherwise it is well hidden in the woods and very difficult to see unless you know exactly where to look. Despite the reported presence of slag around the furnace, I did not find any slag or remnants of iron ore when I looked. At the time of my visit to the site in August 2014, the area was heavily overgrown and virtually all the ground was covered by briars and thick green plants, which likely obscured some of the surface slag. There was also an abundance of spiders and their webs, and it was difficult to walk around the furnace without becoming entangled in spiderwebs and having to constantly brush off spiders.

Generally these iron furnaces produced significant amounts of slag, and it had to be nearby. In the days of these old furnaces, they simply dumped the slag at the spot that offered the least resistance and cost for dumping, and I thought this would have to be on the downgradient side of the furnace near the river. I reasoned that at least some of it had to wash downstream of the furnace. Sure enough, when I walked on the north beach of the river near the furnace, I found some pieces of glassy black slag.

Farther downstream is a large gravel bar, and I thought that slag might also be abundant in this area. After hunting on the gravel bar, I soon found some large weathered rocks that were almost entirely black glass with some green and brown sections. Some of the glass resembles obsidian and has pronounced conchoidal fractures when broken. The slag in the stream is generally weathered but can be distinguished from the other rocks as it appears glassy, even when dusted with mud and abraded by the nearby crystalline rocks in the streambed. Once I determined what it looks like, I soon began to see many pieces of the glassy slag in this gravel bar. Bear in mind that the area is within Patapsco Valley State Park, and all associated restrictions to collecting still apply.

References: Singewald, 1911; Short, 1999

43. Bowie Siderite and Shark Teeth

The creek is rich in iron, and fossils can reportedly be found in the Severn Formation sediments along the bank.

County: Prince George's
Site type: Streambed
Land status: Uncertain, not posted; may be private or park land
Material: Siderite nodules and shark teeth
Host rock: Upper Cretaceous basal Severn Formation
Difficulty: Moderate
Family-friendly: No, as land status is uncertain
Tools: Hammer and small screen
Special concerns: Land status uncertain
Special attractions: Washington, DC
GPS parking: 38°57'48"N / 76°42'43"W
GPS bend in river: 38°57'53"N / 76°42'46"W
Topographic quadrangle: Anacostia, DC–MD

Some of the large rocks in the streambed are rounded siderite concretions.

Finding the site: From US 301 South, take exit 13B/13C for MD 3 North and then take exit 13C toward Belair Drive. Go 0.7 mile and merge onto Melford Boulevard. At the traffic circle, take the third exit onto Science Drive. Go 0.2 mile and turn left (northwest) onto Old Crain Drive. The creek with the siderite and shark teeth is in the valley east of Old Crain Drive. I parked in one of the building parking lots near Old Crain Drive and walked to the creek.

Rockhounding

This is an unusual site in that it is in a developed area but none of the ground is posted against trespassing. It is just west of Patuxent River Park, and is listed as a fossil site in a Maryland Geological Survey publication. There is very limited parking on Old Crain Drive, but I parked in the parking lot of one of the buildings south of the locality and walked to the site. There appeared to be a great deal of small businesses with various clients and customers going in and out, so I did not think that I was in danger of being towed or ticketed, but that possibility is always present when parking in a private lot.

I walked into the valley and the first thing I noticed was very large, rounded concretions, many of which protruded from the creek bed and had a septarian fracture pattern. These were very large siderite nodules. Many of them also protruded from the banks. Most were solid and did not have any additional minerals besides fine-grained siderite, but they were still interesting to find. In parts of the creek, it looks like bowling balls are poking up from the streambed. This is even more striking in the calm sections of the stream that would otherwise be smooth except for the upper hemispheres of the siderite concretions breaking the flat surface of the water.

The fossils at this site are small shark and crocodile teeth that weather from the Upper Cretaceous basal Severn Formation. The teeth are found in a thin bed of compact pale gray sand just above the streambed. I was able to find a single very small tooth just by breaking apart the sand with my hands, and I think I could have found more if I had had a small screen to sift the sand. The sand banks are relatively small, and despite my extensive searching on the surface, I did not see any teeth or other fossils. Screening may be the best tool for this site instead of simply looking at the sand surface, which is often the preferred method when looking for shark teeth on a beach. I soon lost my patience with the sand and tiny teeth, and spent the rest of my time looking for good pieces of siderite.

Reference: Glaser, 1979

Sites 43–45

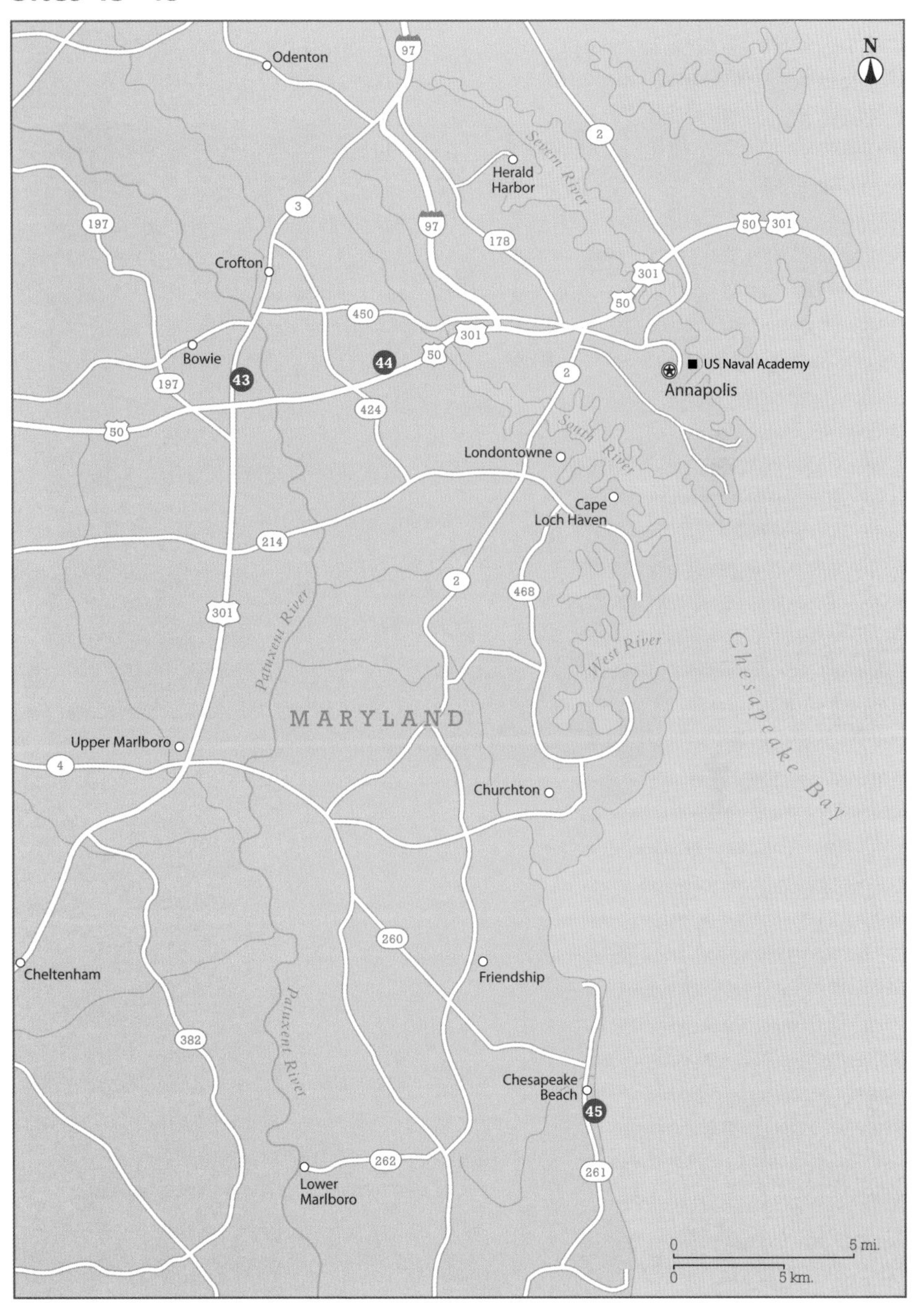

N
Odenton
97
2
Severn River
Herald Harbor
3
197
97
178
50
301
Crofton
301
50
450
301
Bowie
50
44
43
197
2
US Naval Academy
Annapolis
424
50
South River
Londontowne
Cape Loch Haven
214
2
468
301
Patuxent River
West River
Chesapeake Bay
MARYLAND
Upper Marlboro
4
Churchton
260
Friendship
Cheltenham
382
Patuxent River
Chesapeake Beach
45
262
261
Lower Marlboro
0
5 mi.
0
5 km.

44. Tarnans Branch Vivianite Concretions

The concretions are rounded and easy to crack open with a hammer.

See map page 155.

County: Anne Arundel
Site type: Loose rocks along stream sides
Land status: Private, but not posted
Material: Vivianite
Host rock: Middle Eocene Aquia Formation
Difficulty: Difficult
Family-friendly: No
Tools needed: Hammer with pick end for digging concretions from soil
Special concerns: Land status, poison ivy, ticks
Special attractions: None
GPS parking: 38°58'05"N / 76°38'05"W

GPS nodule area: 38°58'04"N / 76°38'07"W
Topographic quadrangle: Bowie, MD
Finding the site: From US 301 North heading east, take exit 16 for MD 424 South. Merge onto MD 424 South and continue 1.2 miles. Turn left (northeast) onto Rutland Road. Continue on Rutland Road for about 1.1 miles, passing back under US 301, and look for a very small parking area on the east side of Rutland Road and just north of Tarnans Branch. This is part of a driveway that turns east and then continues northwest into the woods. The vivianite concretions can be found on the south bank of Tarnans Branch west of Rutland Road.

Rockhounding

The outer layer of the concretions has dark blue vivianite.

This is an obscure site that is described in an *American Mineralogist* article from 1951 by Professor Arthur Barwick, who was a professor of geology at nearby Howard University. Barwick was completing geologic fieldwork for a project with the Office of Naval Research and found large concretionary masses of vivianite exposed in a roadcut along the south bluff of Tarnans Branch where Rutland Road passed beneath the new expressway, US 301. Vivianite is a blue to dark green hydrated iron phosphate, and the color is generally very striking. The concretions were described as 4 to 8 inches wide, deep blue in color, and surrounded by a rusty shell of limonitic material. Barwick felt that the largeness of the concretions and relative abundance was important to mention.

Time and development have obscured most of the area, and the exposures and the concretions would likely have been forgotten long ago if Barwick had not written this short article. However, even when armed with documentation like this, it is far from certain that you can find these old localities. I visited the area in early 2004 to look for the concretions near the expressway but could not find anything.

Upon further review I decided that it would be best to look on the south bank of Tarnans Branch. I was able to park on the east side of Rutland Road and walk upstream on the south side of Tarnans Branch. The ground was not posted and I found evidence that other people entered the area, such as an abandoned fishing tackle box and damaged fishing pole. The area is very heavily overgrown. I walked along the bank and looked at the leaf-covered exposures on the hillsides to the west, but did not find any vivianite. The briars, poison ivy, and mosquitoes were thick, and I was about to give up and write this site off for good. However, as I was walking out, I saw two large gray-green nodules. They looked exactly like the rounded diabase rocks that are very common in the Pennsylvania hills near York. I was about to walk by them, but then realized that diabase would not occur like that in the Atlantic Coastal Plain sediments of Maryland. I immediately cracked one open and found that it had a limonite shell over an intensely deep blue layer of crystalline vivianite. The interior of the rock was also blue, but not as dark as the vivianite in the shell.

These were some of the most unusual rocks I have seen in Maryland. I found another one shortly afterwards, but they seemed to be very rare so I left the rest for other visitors to this site. Some of the concretions were nearly entirely buried in the soil, so I was lucky to find any. Interestingly, I did not see any in the stream, and the south bank appears to be the best place to find them.

Reference: Barwick, 1951

45. Bayfront Park Shark Teeth

The beach is muddy and not great for swimming, but teeth can be found along the shoreline.

See map page 155.
County: Calvert
Site type: Beach
Land status: Public, but parking controlled by Town of Chesapeake Beach
Material: Shark teeth
Host rock: Beach sediments from eroded Miocene Calvert Formation
Difficulty: Easy
Family-friendly: Yes
Tools needed: Small shovel, screen
Special concerns: Cliffs are very unstable, parking during summer is expensive
Special attractions: None
GPS parking: 38°40'41"N / 76°32'07"W
GPS beach: 38°40'41"N / 76°31'56"W

Topographic quadrangle: North Beach, MD
Finding the site: From US 301 South, turn right to merge onto MD 4 South. Continue 6.2 miles and merge onto MD 260 East, then follow MD 260 East for 9 miles. Turn right (south) onto Bayside Road, which is also MD 261. Go 1.2 miles and turn left (east) onto Brownies Beach Road. The parking area is immediately to the right (south). This is an easy turn to miss, and parking is limited so it is best to go early or late in the day.

Rockhounding

This is one of the best places to find shark teeth on the western shore of Chesapeake Bay in Maryland. The beach is reached by a short hike from the parking area. While part of the beach is sandy and suitable for sunbathing, the main attraction is shark teeth, and nearly everyone who visits the beach has a small shovel and screen. The more advanced collectors are easy to spot, as they have larger shovels, rugged screens, and suitable footwear.

The Miocene Calvert Formation is the source of the shark teeth, and the formation is well exposed in the cliffs south of the main beach area. Some of the mudstones exposed along the cliffs and the large broken slabs that have fallen into the water expose casts of bivalves and other fossils. The beach cliffs are constantly eroding, and it is important to stay away from their edges; the Chesapeake Beach Town Council has posted a sign against entering the cliffs area. However, the water is very shallow and it is possible to walk along the beach and stay well away from the cliffs, especially when the tide is low. Several trees have fallen from the cliffs and many of these make it challenging to walk along the beach, but they also provide places for shark teeth to accumulate with the regular tides and frequent winds that hit the beach. The best time for looking for teeth is at low tide after a storm, and it is best to start early in the day, as the obvious teeth that have washed up will be grabbed very quickly. You can use a screen or carefully watch the beach shoreline as the water washes over the beach and brings in new teeth.

We met one collector who was properly equipped, and he and his family had been at the beach since daybreak. His daughter had reportedly found a megaladon tooth, and he had an impressive array of teeth that he had found by digging and screening sand and gravel under the numerous logs and stumps along the shoreline. We found numerous teeth, but most were relatively small, and instead of megaladon fossils I found extremely tiny teeth best described as from dinkydon.*

**Not a real name*

Many shark teeth are also found by going deeper into the water and screening the gravel around stumps and logs.

While this is a great beach for shark teeth (but not for swimming), the parking fees during the summer beach season are excessive. Many years ago this beach was free, but as of 2014 the Town of Chesapeake Beach was charging out-of-county residents $16 per person, with slightly reduced fees for very young kids or senior citizens. North Beach, their neighbor to the north, wanted $15 a person. Parking is limited and I understand their desire to cover costs, but it effectively drives many people, who would likely spend money in town, away from these beaches. I highly recommend this beach for shark teeth, but you may want to come during the off-season when the fees are reportedly not charged.

References: Cleaves et al., 1968; McLennen, 1971

46. Flag Ponds Beach Shark Teeth

Screening is a lot of work, and we found that it was easier to simply walk along the beach and find teeth.

County: Calvert
Site type: Beach
Land status: Flag Ponds Nature Park, operated by Calvert County
Material: Shark teeth, fossil shells and coral, polished quartz pebbles
Host rock: Beach sediments
Difficulty: Easy
Family-friendly: Yes
Tools needed: None, but a screen and shovel can be useful
Special concerns: Patience required
Special attractions: Swimming and fishing at beach
GPS parking: 38°26'48"N / 76°27'30"W
GPS beach: 38°26'56"N / 76°27'09"W
Topographic quadrangle: Cove Point, MD

Finding the site: From US 301 South, turn right to merge onto MD 4 South and go 33.4 miles. Turn left (northeast) toward Flag Ponds Parkway, make a sharp right, and continue on Flag Ponds Parkway for 0.7 mile. Take the first right and go 0.1 mile to the parking area. From here you can walk to Flag Ponds Beach.

The beach is very broad, and shark teeth can be found by watching the shoreline as the water washes them up.

Rockhounding

This is a unique area for finding shark teeth along the western side of Chesapeake Bay, as it is one of the few places that does not have a cliff directly against the beach. Flag Ponds Beach is a broad area of Quaternary lowlands deposits, and the fossils have weathered primarily from the sands and clays of the St. Marys and Choptank Formations.

This site requires patience, but the teeth are there. At first we were shoveling shoreline gravels and sand into a screen and shaking them underwater to see what we could find. We found a lot of fossil coral and some very tiny teeth. Later we watched some experienced collectors, and one of them suggested that we simply walk along the shoreline and watch the water for teeth. They had found many shark teeth along the beach, and one of the teeth that they found actually appeared to be a mammalian molar tooth with the roots. They did not use a screen at all, but simply watched the beach-wave boundary very closely. Once we started simply looking on the surface for black teeth washing ashore, we had much more success. We soon found several more shark teeth, and they were much bigger than the ones we found with the screen. We did not find any mammalian teeth, but were still very pleased with the shark teeth we had found.

A fee is charged for access to Flag Ponds Beach, but it is very reasonable, especially when compared to the city-run beaches to the north. Calvert County is much more tourist-friendly than the Chesapeake shore cities, and I highly recommend coming here instead during the summer season so you do not get taken to the cleaners by beach access fees at city-run beaches. Flag Ponds Beach is also much nicer than the city beaches, especially for swimming and relaxing.

Reference: Cleaves, et al, 1968

Sites 46–49

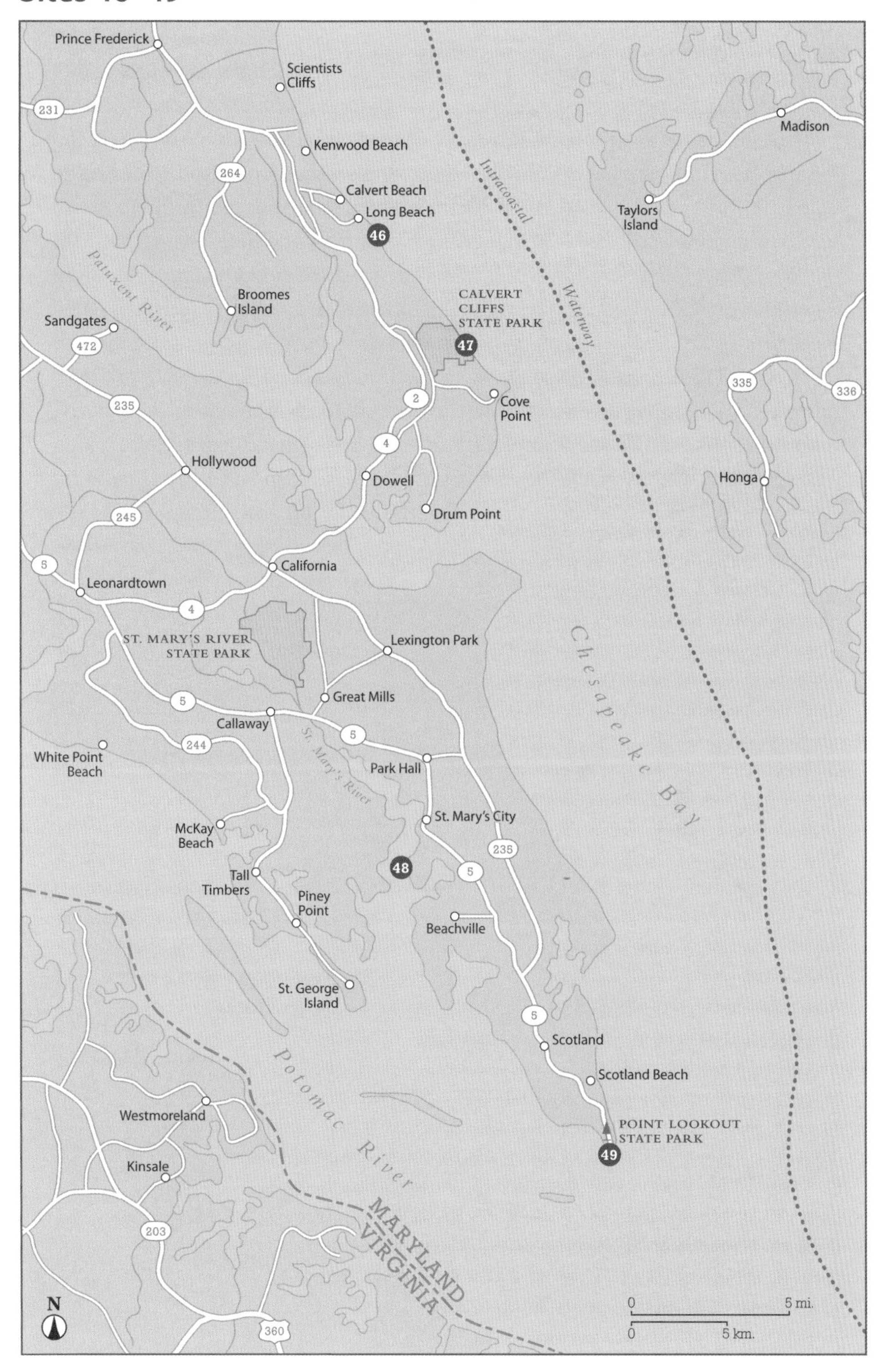

Prince Frederick
Scientists Cliffs
231
Kenwood Beach
264
Calvert Beach
Long Beach
46
Intracoastal
Taylors Island
Madison
Patuxent River
Broomes Island
Sandgates
472
CALVERT CLIFFS STATE PARK
47
Waterway
235
2
Cove Point
335
336
4
Hollywood
Dowell
Honga
Drum Point
245
5
California
Leonardtown
4
ST. MARY'S RIVER STATE PARK
Lexington Park
Chesapeake Bay
Great Mills
5
Callaway
5
244
White Point Beach
Park Hall
St. Mary's River
St. Mary's City
McKay Beach
235
48
5
Tall Timbers
Piney Point
Beachville
St. George Island
5
Scotland
Potomac River
Scotland Beach
Westmoreland
POINT LOOKOUT STATE PARK
49
Kinsale
203
MARYLAND
VIRGINIA
360
N
0
5 mi.
0
5 km.

47. Calvert Cliffs State Park Shark Teeth

Screens as well as a watchful eye can help you find teeth at Calvert Cliffs.

See map page 165.
County: Calvert
Site type: Beach
Land status: Calvert Cliffs State Park
Material: Shark teeth, fossil fragments
Host rock: Beach sediments
Difficulty: Easy
Family-friendly: Yes
Tools needed: Screen, small shovel, sharp eyes
Special concerns: Beach can be very crowded, areas near cliffs likely closed
Special attractions: Pleasant hike to beach, turtle pond
GPS parking: 38°23'48"N / 76°26'07"W

GPS beach: 38°24'11"N / 76°24'29"W
Topographic quadrangle: Cove Point, MD
Finding the site: From US 301 South, turn right to merge onto MD 4 South and go 37.4 miles. Turn left (northeast) to enter Calvert Cliffs State Park. Park in the parking area and follow the hiking trail to the beach. This is a pleasant but long hike.

Rockhounding

Calvert Cliffs extend from Chesapeake Beach in northern Calvert County to Drum Point at the southern end of Calvert County. The cliffs are a prominent feature of the shoreline and expose Miocene sediments, which range from six to twenty million years old. Due to the dip of the formations to the south, the rocks in the northern part of the county are older than the rocks to the south. The oldest formation is the Calvert Formation in the northern end, followed by the younger Choptank Formation, and the youngest of the three, the St. Marys Formation, is exposed in the southern end.

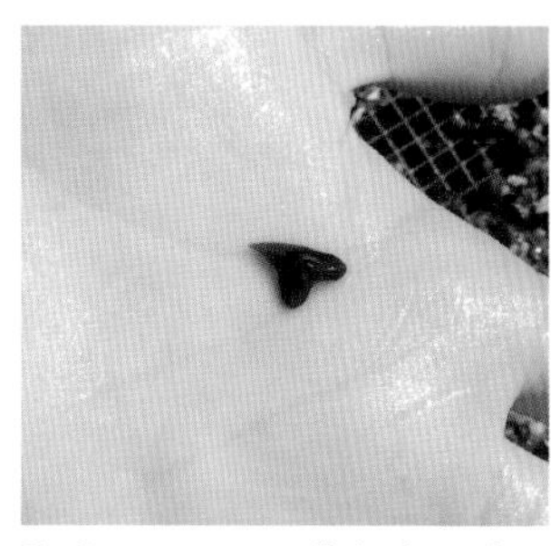

Finding even a small shark tooth is very satisfying when you are screening gravels.

Most of the cliffs are on private property, but Calvert Cliffs State Park is open to the public and you can collect shark teeth on the beach. We hiked to the beach from the parking area in July 2014. It was a very sunny and hot day, and there were a lot people on the beach. The cliffs had been clearly marked as closed, so we stayed away from them. We spent a lot of time screening gravel, but then the park ranger told us that the best way to find teeth was to look on the ground surface. Almost immediately after she said this, she found a tooth next to my foot, and I would have missed it otherwise.

The cliffs and beach are scenic, but they can be crowded. It is best to visit this beach after a storm and during low tide, and come early in the morning if possible. Alternatively, if you come at the peak of high tide, you can be among the first to watch the shoreline as the tide recedes and exposes what was washed up during high tide. There are many other shark teeth collectors on this beach, and they are sure to grab newly washed up shark teeth very quickly. Although it is crowded and a long hike to the beach, it is still an excellent beach for teeth. Be sure to bring plenty of water, as it is a long way back to the car.

Reference: Glaser, 1979

48. Chancellor Point Beach Quartz

The beach at Chancellor Point is sandy and has an abundance of rounded quartz pebbles.

See map page 165.
County: St. Mary's
Site type: Beach
Land status: Chancellor Point Natural History Area
Material: Quartz pebbles
Host rock: Quaternary lowlands sediments
Difficulty: Easy
Family-friendly: Yes
Tools needed: Small plastic bag for pebbles, sharp eyes
Special concerns: Parking is very limited
Special attractions: Fishing in St. Mary's River
GPS parking: 38°10'11"N / 76°26'14"W
GPS picnic area: 38°10'10"N / 76°26'31"W
GPS beach: 38°10'07"N / 76°26'38"W

Topographic quadrangle: St. Mary's City, MD

Finding the site: From the town of Lexington Park, from the intersection of MD 246 and MD 235, head southeast on MD 235 for 4.1 miles. Turn right (west) onto Mattapany Road and go 2.1 miles, then turn left (east) onto MD 5 South, go about 300 feet, and turn right onto Rosecroft Road. Go 1.3 miles and you will come to a turn to the left (south), but it is still Rosecroft Road. Park here and walk to a trail that is on the west side of Rosecroft Road just opposite the intersection with Lucas Cove Road. This trail will take you to the beach, which is about 1,500 feet to the west.

Rockhounding

This is one of the few locations with access to a beach along the St. Mary's River, as most of the surrounding land is private. The beach is reached by a well-marked trail that leads to an area with two picnic tables and a "swim at your own risk" sign. The beach sands have a fair number of rocks and numerous nearly clear, rounded quartz pebbles, which appear similar to "Cape May diamonds." When polished correctly, some of these pebbles may become very clear.

Quartz pebbles that can be further polished, along with shell fragments, are easily found on the beach.

We originally came to this site to look for gypsum crystals. Radiating gypsum crystal clusters are reported to occur in Pleistocene clay deposits 0.25 mile south of Chancellor Point. Unfortunately much of this area is private land, and many of the beaches are lined with huge boulders for protection against shoreline erosion. We were not able to walk farther south from the main beach due to the high tide, but I did notice that some of the shoreline to the south had been scoured and that clay was exposed just below the surface of the water. I did not see any gypsum in this clay, and there were not any cliff exposures along the hillside that I could see.

This is another site that might warrant further exploration by boat or extensive hiking during low tide. If you cannot find gypsum crystals, you will still find some nice beach quartz. Please also note that the collecting status of this area is uncertain. There were no signs prohibiting beachcombing, but many parks, even when they have public access, restrict many activities related to natural resources.

References: Ostrander and Price, 1940; Cleaves et al., 1968

49. Point Lookout Beach Quartz

The riprap provides a convenient place to sit down while you are scanning the beach sands for rounded quartz pebbles.

See map page 165.
County: St. Mary's
Site type: Beach
Land status: Point Lookout State Park
Material: Beach quartz
Host rock: Quaternary lowlands deposits
Difficulty: Easy
Family-friendly: Yes
Tools needed: None
Special concerns: State park; no collecting allowed
Special attractions: Lighthouse, fishing, swimming, Civil War monuments
GPS parking: 38°02'23"N / 76°19'21"W
GPS beach: 38°02'27"N / 76°19'17"W

Topographic quadrangle: Point Lookout, MD
Finding the site: From the town of Lexington Park, from the intersection of MD 246 and MD 235, head southeast on MD 235 for 4.1 miles. Turn right (west) onto Mattapany Road and go 2.1 miles, then turn left (east) onto MD 5 South, continue 3.9 miles, and turn right to stay on MD 5 South. Continue 2.8 miles to the parking area. The beach with the quartz pebbles is about 400 feet to the northeast and is bisected by a pier of large boulders. Many of the other beaches in the area are covered with boulders to protect the coastline from erosion.

Rockhounding

Point Lookout's location at the confluence of the Potomac River and Chesapeake Bay results in well-rounded beach quartz.

Point Lookout is at the southern tip of St. Mary's County and is the southernmost part of Maryland's western shore on Chesapeake Bay. It is at the end of a long peninsula located at the confluence of the Potomac River and Chesapeake Bay. It was a key location to spot ships sailing up the Potomac and Chesapeake, and got the name Point Lookout because American forces used it to watch approaching ships during the Revolutionary War and the War of 1812.

During the Civil War the peninsula was used by the Union Army as a prisoner-of-war camp for Confederate soldiers, and there are many Civil War monuments in the area. Point Lookout also has an old lighthouse, which was built in 1830 and deactivated in 1966. Somehow it got the reputation as the most haunted lighthouse in America, and this designation has undoubtedly increased tourist traffic to Point Lookout and visitors who would normally never bother to see a lighthouse. Fishing is also extremely popular at Point Lookout, and there is a swimming beach on the Potomac side of the peninsula.

The location of Point Lookout at the confluence of the Potomac and Chesapeake, combined with the wave action, has brought a tremendous amount of reworked quartz pebbles and various rocks to the beaches. Some of the quartz pebbles are well-rounded, nearly translucent, and resemble unpolished Cape May diamonds. Unfortunately many of the key beaches with quartz pebbles have been covered by large boulders to protect the shoreline from the unrelenting erosion of the waves. However, there are still some small sections of exposed beaches with abundant pebbles. The best pebble beach that we were able to find is located on the shoreline just east of the main parking area and north of the lighthouse. This beach has an abundance of rounded white quartz pebbles, and the nearby boulders provide a convenient place to sit while you are scanning the surf for the clearest pebbles.

Reference: Eckert, 2000

50. Catoctin Furnace Glassy Slag and Limonite

These mounds have a lot of limonite on the surface, suggesting they are former mine tailings or ore stockpiles.

County: Frederick
Site type: Slag heaps and mine dumps
Land status: Cunningham Falls State Park
Material: Slag and limonite
Host rock: Late Precambrian metasediments
Difficulty: Easy
Family-friendly: Yes
Tools needed: None
Special concerns: State park; no collecting allowed
Special attractions: Cunningham Falls
GPS parking: 39°35'09"N / 77°26'10"W
GPS mine dumps: 39°34'57"N / 77°26'04"W

Topographic quadrangle: Catoctin Furnace, MD
Finding the site: From the Pennsylvania border, follow US 15 South for 11.9 miles. The entrance to Cunningham Falls State Park will be on your right (west). Park here and take the trail from the parking area to the walking bridge over US 15. The slag heaps and former iron mines are in the park east of US 15.

Rockhounding

The slag is vesicular and glassy and can easily be seen from the trail.

The Catoctin Furnace was a major iron furnace that began operation in 1774 and did not finally close until 1903. The furnace produced pig iron and reportedly supplied iron cannonballs for the Revolutionary War. It roasted iron ores obtained from zones of limonite and hematite that formed in nearby late Precambrian metasediments. The furnace was fired by charcoal, and ultimately could no longer compete with the more efficient iron mines that had been developed by the end of the 1800s. The area is now within Cunningham Falls State Park, and remnants of the original slag heaps and mine dumps can be observed from the trails.

The slag and limonite are present on the east side of US 15, and I was not able to find any indications of mines or tailings west of US 15 near the parking area. The park has labeled some of the more prominent slag piles, and a good zone of slag is right next to one of the sets of wooden steps on the trail. The slag heaps are extensive and are primarily glassy gray vesicular slag, but some light blue colors can also be seen in some of the loose slag on the ground. A site map is also provided on one of the historical markers to show the general location of the slag and a former pond and dam that were used to control water flow for the operation.

Near the dam and pond are large red and brown mounds. These appear to be former mining dumps or ore stockpiles, and they have representative examples of the limonite and hematite mineralization. Most of the limonite is dark to light brown, and the hematite is relatively minor when compared to the limonite. Many loose pieces of iron mineralization can also be seen on the trail. However, as this is a state park, collecting rock and minerals is prohibited. Although collecting is not allowed, this is a very good place to learn about the history of early iron furnaces and see abundant glassy slag and some of the original iron minerals.

References: Cleaves et al., 1968; Parish, 1971

Sites 50–55

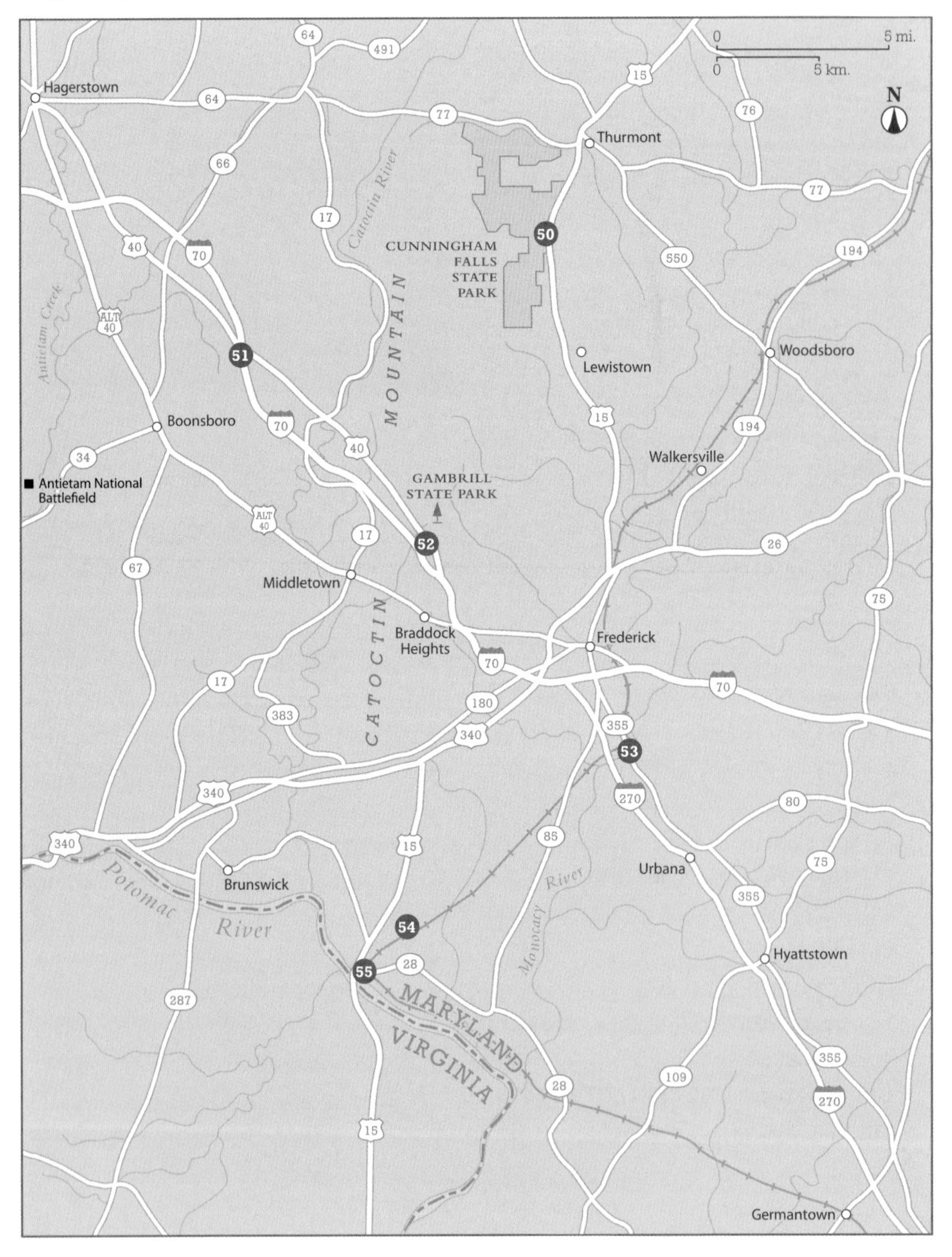

51. Highway 40 Metarhyolite

The metarhyolite is weathered and fractured, and fresh pieces are challenging to find in the outcrop.

See map page 176.
County: Frederick
Site type: Roadcut
Land status: Next to Appalachian Trail parking, not posted
Material: Metarhyolite
Host rock: Precambrian metarhyolite
Difficulty: Easy
Family-friendly: Yes
Tools needed: Hammer with pick end to dig through loose rocks
Special concerns: Traffic next to outcrop
Special attractions: Appalachian Trail
GPS parking: 39°32'08"N / 77°36'14"W
Topographic quadrangle: Meyersville, MD

Finding the site: From US 15 South, take exit 13B and merge onto US 40 West. Continue 13.1 miles and look for the parking area for the Appalachian Trail access to your left. You will almost certainly see several vehicles parked in this area, and you can safely park your car here away from the traffic. The metarhyolite is exposed in a broad roadcut on the south side of US 40 West just east of the Frederick-Washington County border.

Rockhounding

This is a convenient and easily accessed exposure of metarhyolite. The metarhyolite is bedded, and when viewed along the beds, one can see the various colors, which range from reddish brown to light gray to pink. Some of the most colorful pieces are the ones that have been subjected to surface weathering, and these are often found as shiny loose rocks along the side of the highway. The outcrop has some iron staining and many sections are altered to clay minerals, and it is challenging to find fresh exposures of hard metarhyolite.

This small piece of metarhyolite has weakly defined purplish-pink and gray bands.

When I visited this roadcut in August 2014, construction was under way near the US 40 bridge where it crosses I-70, and several orange barrels were placed along the roadcut between the eastbound traffic and the roadcut. This made it much safer to observe this cut, and it appeared that access was being constructed along the roadside to reach the Appalachian Trail. If this is the case, this should continue to be a reasonably safe roadcut to observe, but you still must be very careful of the traffic.

There are additional metarhyolite exposures on US 40 on the next hill to the southeast, just southeast of a state highway facility, but these exposures have a lot of clay and are very soft and platy. Traffic is much more dangerous along this section of US 40 to the southeast, and I recommend wearing an orange safety vest and only visiting this other exposure during periods of light traffic if you insist on checking it out.

References: Cleaves et al., 1968; Means, 2010

52. Highway 40 Catoctin Metabasalt

The Catoctin metabasalt has abundant light green epidote and white quartz veins.

See map page 176.
County: Frederick
Site type: Roadcut
Land status: Uncertain, not posted
Material: Epidote, chlorite, quartz
Host rock: Catoctin metabasalt
Difficulty: Easy
Family-friendly: No; traffic is a significant concern
Tools needed: Hammer
Special concerns: Traffic, especially westbound US 40, and limited parking
Special attractions: Appalachian Trail
GPS parking: 39°27'20"N / 77°30'06"W
Topographic quadrangle: Middletown, MD

Finding the site: From US 15 South, take exit 13B and merge onto US 40 West. Continue 5.2 miles, and you will see the exposures of green metabasalt on both sides of the road. Parking is very limited, but you can find a small pull-off on the shoulder just west of and immediately east of the intersection of Ridge Road with US 40.

Rockhounding

This roadcut along US 40 exposes a long section of Catoctin metabasalt on both sides of the highway just west of the intersection with Ridge Road. I found it safest to stick to observing the outcrop on the south side of the road, as cars approaching from the west are going uphill and a little slower. Checking out the exposures on the westbound part of US 40, which is the north side of the road, exposes you to cars coming from the east and speeding downhill, and they are traveling much faster. A bright orange or yellow safety vest is highly recommended for this site.

The metabasalt is deep to light green and has large veins of white bull quartz, which is solid, milky-white quartz. I had hoped that the quartz veins might have some vugs or zones of crystals, but I did not find any crystals in these veins. The metabasalt has a lot of light green epidote, and some of the coarser sections have green platy minerals that I assume are chlorite. Calcite is also reported to occur in the metabasalt, as well as some zones of amygdaloidal meta-andesite, but I did not see any in my limited time at these outcrops. The

Some of the basalt has veins of what appears to be antigorite.

metabasalt is very dense, and the metamorphism likely served as a mechanism to further compress these rocks that were already rich in iron and magnesium.

Veinlets of fibrous aggregates, which may be antigorite, can also be found in some of the zones that exhibit greater color variation due to the abundance of white quartz, light green epidote, and dark green metabasalt. The greatest concentrations of different minerals are found in these zones.

References: Cleaves et al., 1968; Means, 2010

53. Highway 355 Frederick Limestone

This is a very small outcrop on a busy highway, and you must be extremely careful at this site.

See map page 176.
County: Frederick
Site type: Roadcut
Land status: Monocacy National Battlefield
Material: Solution-weathered limestone
Host rock: Cambrian Frederick limestone
Difficulty: Easy
Family-friendly: No; too much traffic
Tools needed: None; no collecting allowed
Special concerns: Highway traffic, very small outcrop
Special attractions: Monocacy National Battlefield
GPS parking: 39°22'07"N / 77°23'23"W

GPS outcrop: 39°22'06"N / 77°23'23"W
Topographic quadrangle: Buckeystown, MD–VA
Finding the site: From I-70, take exit 54 for MD 85 South, go about 3.5 miles, and turn left (south) onto MD 355 South. Go 2.3 miles and immediately after you cross the Monocacy River bridge, park in the parking area on the east side of the road. The outcrop of Frederick limestone is right across the road. This is a very busy highway, and you should wear a safety vest and be extremely careful when looking at this outcrop.

The weathered Frederick limestone resembles bark from a ponderosa pine tree.

Rockhounding

This outcrop is an excellent example of solution weathering in a limestone. The Frederick limestone at this location is very jagged, which is caused by the differential weathering of the limestone. Zones with a higher proportion of calcium carbonate weather faster than zones with a higher proportion of clays. The outcrop reminded me of the bark from a ponderosa pine tree. This is a very small outcrop, and since it is within the Monocacy National Battlefield, no collecting is allowed.

I took a brief walk along the Monocacy River and some of the nearby trails, but did not see any similar exposures of the Frederick limestone. As it is soft and relatively easy to weather, it generally forms valleys and lowlands in the region, and large exposures can be difficult to find. This site is worth a brief visit since it is an unusual outcrop and easy to access, but you must be very careful on the roadside, and its location makes it very dangerous to visit with children or large groups. It would be interesting to find similar larger exposures of Frederick limestone along the Monocacy River or other nearby areas, as this solution weathering is very unusual looking, and it would be good to find an outcrop where you do not have to constantly worry about being hit by a car.

Reference: Means, 2010

54. Ballenger Creek Road Potomac Marble

The rocks can easily be accessed from the roadside.

See map page 176.
County: Frederick
Site type: Roadcut and outcrop
Land status: Private, not posted
Material: Limestone conglomerate
Host rock: Triassic New Oxford Formation
Difficulty: Easy
Family-friendly: Yes
Tools needed: Hammer
Special concerns: Land and access status uncertain, ticks
Special attractions: C&O Canal National Historic Park
GPS parking: 39°17'38"N / 77°30'44"W

Topographic quadrangle: Point of Rocks, MD–VA

Finding the site: Head south on US 15/US 340 from Frederick, Maryland. Take the slight left to Leesburg, Virginia, to stay on US 15 South and continue 5.8 miles to a traffic circle. Take the third exit onto Point of Rocks Road, go 0.2 mile, and turn left (north) onto MD 351. Proceed 1.2 miles and look for a substation on your left. Park on the right (east) side of the road in an unpaved area. The outcrops are on both sides of the road.

Rockhounding

Potomac marble has considerable variability in clast size and type, and this generally made it a poor choice for building stone.

This is a very accessible location to see "Potomac marble," which is a multicolored limestone conglomerate of the Triassic New Oxford Formation. It is also known as calico rock or Potomac breccia. It was used for the rock columns in the old US House of Representatives building in Washington, DC, which is now Statuary Hall. The stone was quarried in Frederick County along the Potomac River near Washington Junction. Although it was colorful, the stone was difficult to cut and carve, as the clasts and matrix of the conglomerate varied in hardness. Many of the pebbles in the matrix undoubtedly popped out at inconvenient times and locations, and this would lead to holes and weakened structures. Even so, at least one company intermittently continued to extract Potomac marble as late as 1898.

The substation is clearly off-limits, but there is an abundance of loose rocks and outcrops on both sides of Ballenger Creek Road at this site. The limestone clasts are gray to white and cemented together by a matrix of fine-grained brownish-orange to reddish-pink calcium carbonate. Large exposures are also present along the power line easement to the southeast. This ground is not posted and it appeared that many people walk into this area, but I confined nearly all of my time at this site to the roadcut. I was at the site in June 2014, and was literally covered with ticks after walking in the grass near the outcrops along the road. Strong bug spray and light-colored clothes are definitely recommended for this location.

References: Cleaves et al., 1968; Kuff and Brooks, 1985; Means, 2010

55. Point of Rocks Goethite and Limonite

Brookshire Run can be reached by the trail from the parking area, and the creek bed has abundant limonite and goethite.

See map page 176.

County: Frederick

Site type: Streambed, former mine trenches

Land status: Point of Rocks Community Park

Material: Goethite and limonite nodules

Host rock: Clayey fault zone between Harpers and Loudoun Formations

Difficulty: Easy

Family-friendly: Yes, as access is relatively good

Tools needed: Hammer

Special concerns: Signs indicate woods are a "Forest Retention" area, collecting status uncertain

Special attractions: Harpers Ferry National Historical Park

GPS parking: 39°16'37"N / 77°32'12"W
GPS bridge over Brookshire Run: 39°16'43"N / 77°32'09"W
Topographic quadrangle: Point of Rocks, MD–VA
Finding the site: Head south on US 15/US 340 from Frederick, Maryland. Take the slight left to Leesburg, Virginia, to stay on US 15 South and continue 5.8 miles to a traffic circle. Take the third exit onto Point of Rocks Road, go 0.2 mile, and turn right (southwest) onto Ballenger Creek Pike. Continue 0.8 mile and turn left (east) onto Tuck Avenue. Go 0.1 mile and turn left into the parking lot for Point of Rocks Community Park. Follow the trail to the north, which crosses Brookshire Run. From here you can walk upstream and observe limonite nodules and fragments in the streambed and weathering out of the stream banks.

Rockhounding

Point of Rocks is named for the prominent outcrop of rocks along the east side of the Potomac River just northwest of town. However, you cannot see the rocks from Point of Rocks, and when driving into this small town, it is hard to imagine that this was a former iron-mining area.

Iron ores were mined from the Point of Rocks area from the late 1700s to mid-1800s. The iron occurred as masses of goethite that formed in a fault zone between the Harpers and Loudoun Formations. The goethite also reportedly occurs with massive milky white quartz. The ores were extracted from trenches near the center of the town. Like most mines in the region, development has covered much of the former mining activity, but fortunately the town has preserved a significant amount of open space through Point of Rocks Community Park. This is a well-maintained park with soccer fields and a paved trail, which crosses Brookshire Run. Brookshire Run is a small tributary of the Potomac River. The park managers have done an excellent job with preserving the park, and it appears to be a very safe place for walking and looking at the remaining iron mineralization, but access into the woods may be questionable.

The woods surrounding the park have signs that indicate the area is a "Forest Retention" area, and this prohibits storage, dumping, or other disturbance in the woods. I am not sure if walking off the path into the woods qualifies as disturbance, but you have to keep this in mind. Brookshire Run has several small paths to access the stream, and I walked along the stream to look for pieces of goethite, as it appeared others regularly walk along the creek. I immediately found some large dense fragments with goethite, and saw large iron nodules with limonite and minor hematite in the short cliffs that form the stream banks, especially at bends in the creek that would undercut the soils and weathered bedrock.

This geothite-rich rock was found in Brookshire Run.

Just east of the trail to Brookshire Run are several large overgrown trenches in the woods. These appeared to be the former mine trenches and pits. I found some small pieces of goethite in these pits, but they have been picked nearly clean of obvious mineralization, and the thick leaf cover and briars prevented me from directly observing the bedrock. The best place to find the goethite and limonite appears to be in Brookshire Run. Since this is a park, collecting status is uncertain, so it is best to assume that collecting is not allowed, even though there are no signs prohibiting mineral or rock collecting at the park. I would also be careful to avoid unwanted attention if you walk into the "Forest Retention" area, as you never know if a local police officer or park authorities will see this as an opportunity to stick an out-of-towner with a big fine.

References: Cleaves et al., 1968; Bernstein, 1980

56. McCoys Ferry Devonian Fossils

The fossils are found in the shale beneath the railroad bridge.

County: Washington
Site type: Roadcut/exposures beneath railroad bridge
Land status: Chesapeake & Ohio Canal National Historical Park
Material: Brachiopods
Host rock: Devonian Hamilton Group shale
Difficulty: Easy
Family-friendly: Yes
Tools needed: None
Special concerns: National historical park; no collecting allowed
Special attractions: Chesapeake & Ohio Canal National Historical Park
GPS parking: 39°36'32"N / 77°58'13"W
Topographic quadrangle: Hedgesville, WV–MD

Finding the site: Heading northwest on I-70 West, take exit 18 and merge onto MD 68 West. Follow this for 0.7 mile, then turn left onto US 40 West and go 0.5 mile. Turn left onto Boyd Road, go 2.8 miles, and turn right onto MD 56 West. Go 0.5 mile and turn left onto McCoys Ferry Road. Go about 0.9 mile and take the fork to the right, which takes you underneath a railroad bridge. The fossils are found in the rocks exposed beneath the bridge.

Rockhounding

McCoys Ferry is located at Mile 110.4 in the Chesapeake & Ohio National Historical Park. This was one of the numerous ferries that crossed the Potomac, and it was the site of a Civil War battle in 1861 and a crossing of the Potomac by Confederate troops in 1862. Like many former battlefields, today it is very peaceful, and it is hard to comprehend what happened here and what it must have looked like during the Civil War.

This site is a good example of how you can often find fossil-bearing outcrops by simply being observant. I had originally tried to access the site that is listed as "Site 21" in Jasper Burns's fossil book and as the "Devonian Crinoid locality near Big Spring" in Glaser's book on Maryland fossil localities. Unfortunately this site is on private land and was clearly marked against trespassing, so it was not possible to visit.

I wrote this private site off and drove south on McCoys Ferry Road to see if there might be any Devonian outcrops near the C&O Canal. As you drive south you enter into the national historical park, so while collecting is

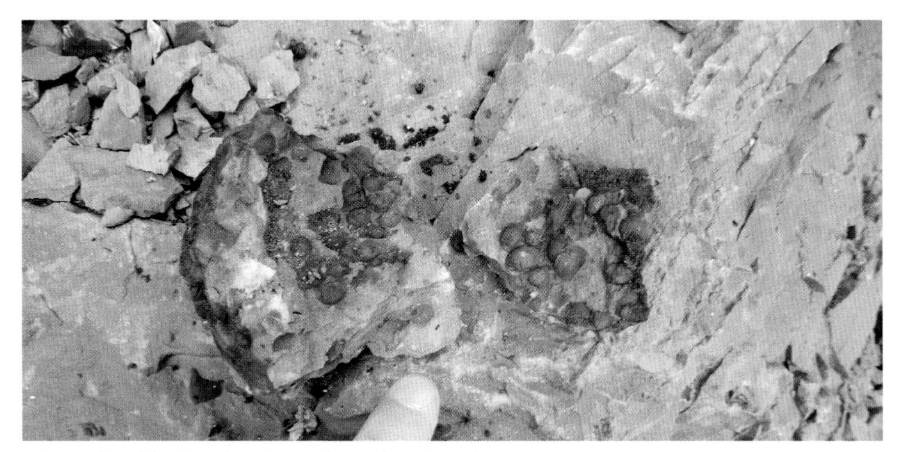

This small rock had an abundance of small brachiopods.

not allowed, at least you can visit the area and look at the rocks. On the way to the canal, I took a side road that passed under the railroad bridge. A large outcrop of shale and talus is at the base of this bridge, and it has many loose rocks and exposed sections that have Devonian brachiopods and crinoids. It is possible to safely park right next to the outcrop, and since this is a side road, it does not get much traffic.

Although collecting is not allowed, it is still an excellent place to see Devonian fossils, and makes a good side trip if you are visiting this section of the C&O Canal. This road does not get much visitor traffic but the area is regularly patrolled by park police, and you will want to make sure that if you observe the outcrop, you are not perceived as collecting or disturbing any of the fossils.

References: Cleaves et al., 1968; Glaser, 1979; Burns, 1991

Sites 56–60

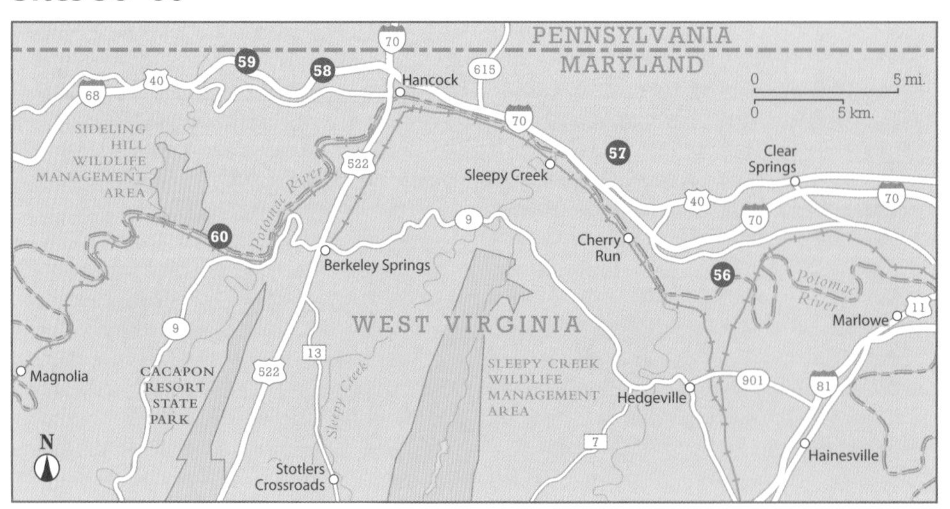

57. Pecktonville Devonian Brachiopods

The most abundant fossils are found in this nondescript section of the trail between the cabin and the old concrete foundations.

See map page 192.
County: Washington
Site type: Loose rocks along hillside
Land status: Camp Harding County Park and adjacent private land
Material: Brachiopods
Host rock: Lower Devonian Keyser limestone
Difficulty: Easy
Family-friendly: Yes, but land status questionable
Tools needed: Hammer
Special concerns: Mosquitoes, poison ivy, ticks, land status
Special attractions: Fishing along Licking Creek
GPS parking: 39°40'12"N / 78°02'28"W

GPS fossil area: 39°40'14"N / 78°02'13"W
Topographic quadrangle: Cherry Run, WV–MD–PA
Finding the site: From I-70 West, take exit 12 toward Indian Springs. Merge onto MD 56 West (which actually goes northeast here), go 1.4 miles, and turn left (west) onto US 40 West. Go 2.9 miles and turn right (north) onto Pectonville Road (note that the spelling is different from Pecktonville). Go 1.1 miles and take a slight right onto Licking Creek Road. This takes you into Camp Harding Park. Park near the fishing access area, and follow the trail on the north bank of Licking Creek to the fossil locality.

Rockhounding

Camp Harding County Park was used by President Warren G. Harding, Thomas Edison, Henry Ford, and Harvey Firestone for camping and fishing in the 1920s. It is now part of the Washington County Parks system and a relatively modern park with excellent access and parking.

When I visited this site in May 2014, it was during extremely high water on Licking Creek. The trail along the creek was nearly submerged and very muddy, but it soon climbed a little higher and away from the creek. I assumed the trail was for fishing access to the creek, as there is a property immediately

This loose rock had large brachiopod exposed on its surface.

to the north that is posted against trespassing, and I did not encounter any further posted signs along the trail. As you hike eastward on this trail, you will pass a small cabin. Just before you reach some old concrete foundations, you can find fossils along the trail. The trail gets very faint here, and it is quite overgrown with vegetation. The fossils are mainly brachiopods that are in partially silicified sandy limestone of the Keyser Formation. The fossil-bearing rocks are generally light tan to light brown, and while some fossils are clearly visible on weathered surfaces, a hammer is useful to crack them open to expose fossil-bearing sections. I found that the best fossils are the large rocks that are found on the trail, and I was not able to find any outcrops with fossils.

I walked farther east well past the concrete foundations to see if any additional fossil-bearing zones were present along the hillside, but I did not find any more fossils. A review of the geologic map of the region indicates that the formations in this area are nearly vertical and strike nearly north–south, so walking east or west would likely result in heading out of the fossil-bearing zones in the rocks. This also suggests that any fossil-bearing zones are likely to be very narrow, so if you find any good fossiliferous zones, it may be best to focus on them, and if you explore any further, to move north up the hillside or south to the creek, instead of east or west along the trail.

By this time the mosquitoes were becoming a real problem, and this undoubtedly was a result of the high water that flooded the low areas north of Licking Creek. This turned the area into a swamp and mass-produced mosquitoes. Bring bug spray, long pants, and gloves to this site, as it is a site that is well on its way to reverting back to nature.

References: Cleaves et al., 1968; Glaser, 1979

58. Sandy Mile Road Devonian Brachiopods and Gastropods

The quarry has abundant loose white sand and large outcrops of white sandstone.

See map page 192.

County: Washington
Site type: Roadcut
Land status: Private, not posted
Material: Devonian brachiopods and gastropods
Host rock: Devonian Ridgely sandstone and Keyser limestone
Difficulty: Easy
Family-friendly: Yes
Tools needed: Hammer
Special concerns: Land status questionable, traffic along roadside
Special attractions: None
GPS parking: 39°42'44"N / 78°13'49"W

Topographic quadrangle: Hancock, MD–WV–PA

Finding the site: From I-70 West, take exit 1B to merge onto US 522 South. Go 0.6 mile and take the exit toward MD 144. Go 0.1 mile and take a sharp right (north) onto Limestone Road. Go 0.1 mile and turn left (west) onto Creek Road. Go 2.6 miles and turn left (south) onto Sandy Mile Road. Cross over I-68, and the parking area is on the right (north) side of the road. The outcrops are on the south side of the road, and the former sand quarry is immediately to the east and is reached by a very short trail from the road.

Rockhounding

This is a well-known fossil locality in western Maryland, and Sandy Mile Road almost certainly got its name from the abundance of sand at the former quarry near the parking area. The roadcut immediately south of the parking area is an exposure of Ridgely sandstone, which is part of the Oriskany Group. The roadcut is full of molds and casts of brachiopods and gastropods. Some of the outcrops are almost entirely composed of fossil casts, and they

The roadcut next to Sandy Mile Road has abundant fossils.

are extremely hard and difficult to break off with a hammer. Some of the best fossils are found in loose rocks at the base of the outcrop.

The former quarry has a sandy section of Ridgely sandstone, and much of this is weathered to crumbling coarse white sand. Keyser limestone is also reportedly exposed in this quarry. Fossils are reported in the quarry, but I did not find any in this area, just lots and lots of white sand and vertically dipping beds of Ridgely sandstone. There are indications that many other people visit this area. I even found a small plastic children's shovel that was better suited for digging in the sand at the beach. Given the abundance and quality of the white sand in this former quarry, it is not surprising that one would give their kid a plastic beach shovel when visiting this site.

References: Cleaves et al., 1968; Glaser, 1979

59. Sideling Hill Roadcut

The Sideling Hill roadcut is one of largest highway rock exposures in the eastern United States.

See map page 192.

County: Washington
Site type: Very large roadcut
Land status: Maryland Department of Transportation
Material: Section of Devonian through Mississippian sediments
Host rock: Rockwell and Purslane Formations
Difficulty: Easy
Family-friendly: Yes
Tools needed: None; view from a distance only
Special concerns: None
Special attractions: None
GPS parking: 39°43'08"N / 78°16'49"W
Topographic quadrangle: Bellegrove, MD–PA–WV

Finding the site: From I-70 West, take exit 1A to merge onto I-68 West. Continue 6.2 miles and take the exit that leads to the rest area. Park here and walk up the steps and across the footbridge to see the Sideling Hill roadcut.

Rockhounding

No modern book about rocks in Maryland is complete without mentioning the Sideling Hill roadcut. This is an absolutely massive cut through Sideling Hill that exposes a thick synclinal sequence of Devonian through Mississippian sediments. It is one of the largest highway exposures of sedimentary rocks in the northeastern United States. If you look at old topographic maps of the area, you can see what a task it was to cut a pass through Sideling Hill, which is not really a hill, but a very long northeast–southwest trending mountain that extends through Maryland, Pennsylvania, and West Virginia. Going around the mountain was not feasible, and a tunnel would have been extremely expensive and ultimately much more dangerous for travelers on the highway.

The rocks form a prominent syncline that is easy to see from the footbridge across I-68.

Excavation started in April 1983 and was finished sixteen month later in August 1984. The finished highway was opened in August 1985. The cut is 340 feet deep from the crest to the ridge to the level of the highway. No serious accidents or fatalities occurred during the construction of the cut and the highway, which is a credit to the construction firms and the state of Maryland. If a highway through Sideling Hill were to be built today, it would be all but impossible with the environmental permitting requirements and much higher cost of modern equipment and labor.

The exposed rocks consist of the Devonian through Mississippian Rockwell Formation and the Mississippian Purslane Formation. The rocks form a large syncline, which is where the rocks are folded and the beds are concave upward, with the younger rocks in the core of the fold. This is an example where the younger rocks in the core of the syncline are more resistant than the older rocks, and this has led to a classic case topographic inversion, where rocks that were once lower in elevation are now higher in elevation due to erosion.

The Maryland Geological Survey and Maryland Department of Transportation built the Sideling Hill Exhibit Center at the site, which opened in August 1991. During trips through Maryland, I always stopped at the rest area at Sideling Hill and made it a point to visit the exhibit center. My last stop was in 2008, and every time I stopped since then the center was closed, leading me to wonder when it would open again. I only recently learned that it was permanently closed in 2009 due to a lack of funds, which explains why it was always closed when I stopped at the rest area.

Apparently the Sideling Hill Exhibit Center is another long-term casualty of the Great Recession. They have moved the museum to a nearby town, but you have to travel off the highway to see it, and it is not the same as stopping on the interstate and seeing the huge roadcut and the museum together. However, you can still walk up to the viewing platform and cross the footbridge to the south side of I-68. Hopefully they will keep this access open for future travelers on the interstate.

References: Brezinski, 1989; Reger and Conkwright, 2005

60. Woodmont Station Devonian Brachiopods

The rockfall with fossils is near the center of the photograph and to the left of the paved trail.

See map page 192.
County: Washington
Site type: Outcrops along rail trail
Land status: Western Maryland Rail Trail
Material: Brachiopods
Host rock: Devonian Mahantango Formation
Difficulty: Moderate
Family-friendly: Yes
Tools needed: None
Special concerns: Maryland DNR land; no collecting allowed
Special attractions: Hiking/biking along trail
GPS parking: 39°37'42"N / 78°17'54"W

GPS rockfall with brachiopods: 39°37'39"N / 78°17'48"W
Topographic quadrangle: Bellegrove, MD–PA–WV
Finding the site: Head west on I-68 and take exit 77 for US 40. Go 0.3 mile and turn left (south) across I-68 to MD 144 East. Continue on MD 144 East for about 600 feet and turn right (south) onto Woodmont Road. Go 6.3 miles and turn left (east) onto Pearre Road. Continue about 0.5 mile to a gate along the rail trail. Park here and walk east on the trail to the fossil-bearing outcrop on the north side of the trail. This is near the Woodmont Station for the former railroad.

Rockhounding

This is an interesting section of the Devonian Mahantango Formation, as virtually all the beds are vertical and they are very well exposed along the north side of the rail trail. As it is Maryland DNR land, collecting is not allowed, but it is still possible to look at the fossils. The rocks along the trail to the west of the Mahantango are shales and siltstones of the Devonian Braillier Formation, and these do not contain fossils, so do not spend time looking for fossils west of the parking area.

This brachiopod was found in loose rocks near the base of the rockfall.

Collecting in the Mahantango shale requires patience, a watchful eye, and luck. The key is to find the rocks with indications of fossiliferous zones. Many sections of the Mahantango are barren, massive shales and siltstones, and you do not want to waste your time in these areas. Look for indications of fossils that are exposed on the sides of the rocks, such as shell patterns, small voids, less dense rock, or other indications outside of the normal appearance of barren shale and siltstone. I looked all along the section exposed along the rail trail before I found an area that contains fossils. This is a rockfall with an abundance of talus. Although this area has fossils, they are still somewhat few and far between, and the fossils that I found were nearly all brachiopods. Due to the vertical dips of the beds, any fossil-bearing zones are likely to be exposed in only narrow sections along the trail.

After I was done at the rail trail, I searched for reported fossils in the roadcuts approximately 5 miles north on Woodmont Road, but all of the shale and siltstone in these areas was barren. The roadcuts are also quite dangerous due to the traffic on this road. Based on my observations, the best fossil hunting in the Woodmont Station area is definitely along the rail trail at the rockfall.

Reference: Glaser, 1979

61. Corriganville Silurian-Devonian Crinoids and Brachiopods

These light brown rocks in the talus slope often have brachiopods.

County: Allegany
Site type: Railroad cut
Land status: Uncertain, along bicycle route
Material: Crinoids and brachiopods
Host rock: Lower Helderberg Group and upper Keyser limestone
Difficulty: Moderate
Family-friendly: Yes
Tools needed: Hammer
Special concerns: Land and collecting status uncertain; long hike to site
Special attractions: None
GPS parking: 39°40'39"N / 78°48'19"W
GPS fossil area: 39°41'28"N / 78°47'21"W

Topographic quadrangle: Cumberland, MD–PA–WV

Finding the site: From I-68 West, take exit 40 for MD 658/Vocke Road. Turn left (north) and go 0.2 mile, then turn right (northeast) onto US 40 Alt East. Go 1.5 miles and turn left (north) onto Long Drive, which soon turns into Cash Valley Road. Continue on this for 1.6 miles, and the parking area for access to the bike trail along the rail line is to your left (northwest). Park here and walk approximately 1.3 miles to the sharp bend in the rail line/bike path. Cumberland Bone Cave is also at this bend and is a useful reference point. The fossils are found in the talus of the railroad cut at and near the sharp bend.

Rockhounding

This is a scenic fossil locality on US Bicycle Route 50, which lies along the Great Allegheny Passage rail trail. This trail, however, still has an active rail line, so you must be extremely careful with trains.

This piece of limestone had abundant crinoids and was found near the base of the hill near the Cumberland Bone Cave.

The formations exposed at the bend include the lower Helderberg Group and the upper Keyser limestone, and range from Upper Silurian to Lower Devonian. These rocks formed from shallow marine sediments, and limestone makes up most of the rocks. The limestone also has some beds of chert. Crinoids are on some of the weathered surfaces of the limestone, and the crinoid columns are best seen in cross-section where they protrude from the limestone. On the west side of the bend, brachiopods can be found in the sandy limestone talus, and the fossils are best seen on weathered surfaces. The fossils are found between the rail trail and the hillside, and you should be very careful of poison ivy that often grows along the borders of the talus slope.

This site is unique, as it also hosts the Cumberland Bone Cave. The cave was discovered in 1912 when the railroad was being built along the mountain. It extended more than 100 feet downward and had horizontal chambers that extended several hundred feet to another opening on the hillslope. The cave contained an abundance of Pleistocene-era vertebrate fossils, including saber-toothed cats, peccaries, and extinct elephants. The cave is still occasionally excavated but is currently closed by a locked gate and posted against trespassing. It is interesting how this site can be known for both Silurian-Devonian invertebrates and Pleistocene vertebrates.

References: Glaser, 1979; Norden, 2006

Sites 61–63

Grantsville
Frostburg
Corriganville
La Vale
Cumberland
Flintstone
Midland
Lonaconing
Potomac Park
Rawlings
Old Town
Westernport
Keyser
Limestone
Fort Ashby
Meadow Mountain
SAVAGE RIVER STATE FOREST
Savage River Reservoir
Bloomington Lake
Dans Mountain
KNOBLY MOUNTAIN
Martin Mountain
Warrior Mountain
Polish Mountain
River Mountain
MARYLAND
WEST VIRGINIA
N
0 5 mi.
0 5 km.

62. Hoffman Hill Strip Mine Pennsylvanian Plant Fossils

Plant fossils can be found on the side walls of the former strip mine.

See map page 208.
County: Allegany
Site type: Former coal strip mine
Land status: Uncertain, not posted
Material: Pennsylvanian plant fossils
Host rock: Pennsylvanian shales
Difficulty: Moderate
Family-friendly: Yes
Tools needed: Hammer, screwdriver to help split rocks
Special concerns: Land status uncertain, somewhat remote area
Special attractions: None
GPS parking: 39°37'50"N / 78°54'58"W

GPS strip mine cut with plant fossils: 39°37'53"N / 78°54'45"W
Topographic quadrangle: Frostburg, MD–PA
Finding the site: Head west on I-68 and take exit 34 for MD 36. Turn left onto MD 36 South and go 0.3 mile. Turn left into a small parking lot, which appears to be a park-and-ride lot. Park here and hike on the dirt road to the east, and this will take you to the strip mine, which is directly beneath the power lines that cross the area.

Rockhounding

This site is a former strip mine where coal was removed from Pennsylvanian sediments. It has been inactive for several years at minimum, as the area is overgrown with vegetation and there are no signs of recent earth moving. I walked about a mile east of the main pit to see if I could find any fresh mine spoils and fossils, but could not find any signs of recent mining or fossils. There is also a large barren area east of the strip mine pit, and I found some fossil stems, but I could not find many fossils in this area.

The best place to collect is on the north bank of the former strip mine. This area has lots of reddish-gray shale that can be split, and fossils are sometimes found on broken surfaces. I found a very nice fossil leaf in this area, as well as lots of carbonized stems. The fossil impressions are generally black patterns on weathered and broken surfaces, and you will find that you may split many rocks before you find a good fossil.

Reference: Glaser, 1979

This stem and leaf fossil were found by splitting open lot of rocks.

63. Dawson Devonian Fossils

As of 2014, the gas station at this site was closed.

See map page 208.
County: Allegany
Site type: Hillside cut
Land status: Private; closed convenience store/gas station
Material: Devonian fossils
Host rock: Devonian Mahantango Formation
Difficulty: Moderate
Family-friendly: No, as current access is questionable
Tools needed: Hammer, but many rocks are also loose
Special concerns: Business is now closed, access questionable
Special attractions: None
GPS parking: 39°29'09"N / 78°56'34"W
Topographic quadrangle: Keyser, WV–MD

This piece with brachiopods was found in a small drainage on the hillside.

Finding the site: From I-68 West, take exit 42 for US 220 South. Continue on US 220 South for 14.7 miles. The site is on the hillside next to Dale's Pit Stop, which was a gas station and closed as of July 2014.

Rockhounding

This is "Site 32" in Jasper Burns's book on fossil collecting in the mid-Atlantic states. The locality has an exposure of Devonian Mahantango sediments and reportedly has corals and associated reef fossils. It is next to a former business known as Dale's Pit Stop, which was a small convenience store and gas station. The store was closed and abandoned at the time I stopped by the locality in July 2014, so it was not possible to ask the station operator for permission to dig fossils. However, the land on the south side of the station near the exposed rocks was not posted, and I confined my activity at the site to looking at the outcrops and loose rocks on the ground.

Reef complexes in the Mahantango can be interesting fossil localities, as fossils are often abundant and contain corals as well as bivalve fossils. The description by Burns indicated that much of the rock was made of the reef complex, so I thought it would be very easy to see the corals. Unfortunately, at the time of my visit, the exposures were heavily overgrown with grass and brush. I found a loose sandy rock in one of the small drainages on the hillside that had an abundance of brachiopods, but I did not find any corals. I walked along the parking lot looking at the exposures, but all I could see were barren layers of shale and siltstone. Apparently the reef section of the exposure was covered by vegetation, and I was not able to see the key fossil zones.

Although I did not find much at this site, it will undoubtedly return to another use at some point, which may or may not be a gas station. The hillside may then be cleared or excavated, and the fossils may be exposed again at that time. Visiting the site in winter or other times when the vegetation has gone dormant may also reveal the area of the reef and associated coral fossils.

References: Cleaves, 1968; Burns, 1991

WASHINGTON, DC METROPOLITAN AREA

Paint Branch, northeast of Washington, DC (Site 75). The DC area has rockhounding sites that range from heavily developed urban areas to remote beaches along the Potomac River.

Washington, DC

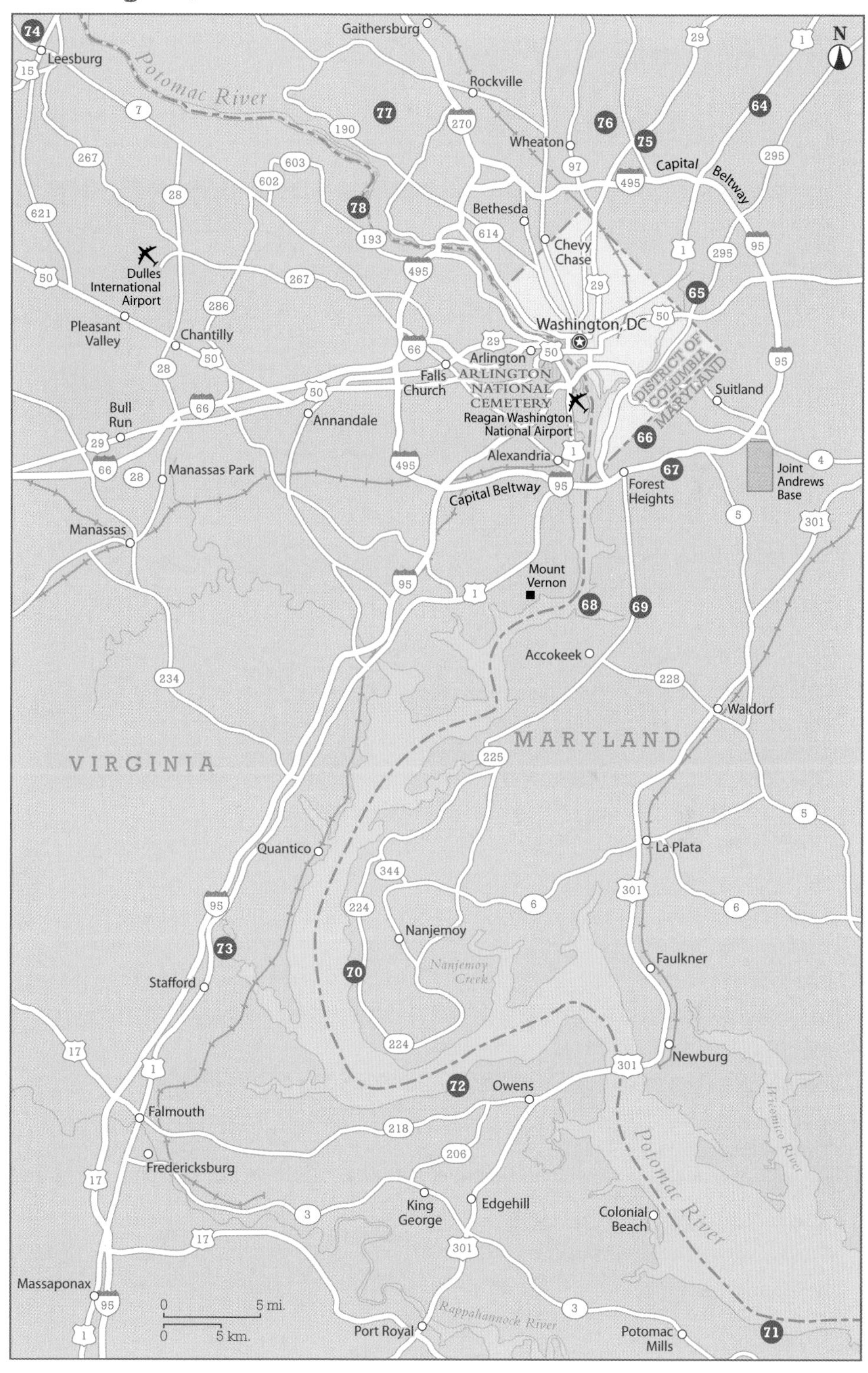

64. Muirkirk Clay Pits Dinosaur Park

Scanning the ground surface is the best way to find fossils at this site.

See map page 221.
County: Prince George's
Site type: Former clay mine
Land status: Dinosaur Park, operated by Prince George's County
Material: Lignite, fossil cones, fossil teeth
Host rock: Clays of Lower Cretaceous Potomac Group
Difficulty: Easy
Family-friendly: Yes
Tools needed: None
Special concerns: No digging allowed
Special attractions: Washington, DC
GPS parking: 39°04'15"N / 76°52'05"W

Topographic quadrangle: Laurel, MD
Finding the site: Head southwest on MD 295 South and exit onto MD 197 North/ Laurel Bowie Road. Go 1.2 miles and turn left (west) onto Contee Road. Go 0.9 mile and turn left (southwest) onto Mid-Atlantic Boulevard. Dinosaur Park is at the southwest end of this road. Park here for the park. This is also one of the few sites in the book that actually has a street address, and it is 13201 Mid-Atlantic Blvd., Laurel, MD 20708. Mid-Atlantic Boulevard is a relatively new road, and will not be listed in GPS units that do not have updated maps.

Rockhounding

The Muirkirk clay pits got their start as iron mines. Siderite, limonite, and hematite nodules found in the clays of the Lower Cretaceous Potomac Group were roasted to produce iron. An iron furnace was built at the site in 1847, and iron ores were processed until 1916. The Muirkirk iron ores had a high manganese content, which gave the iron great tensile strength, and this made the continued mining of these ores economic. However, by 1916 the Muirkirk furnace closed, and it was the last furnace to process Maryland iron ores. After iron mining and processing ceased, the pits were then mined for clay to make bricks, and some of the more colorful iron ores were used to make paint pigment. This continued up to the last part of the twentieth century, and the pits are no longer mined for clay or pigments.

In the 1880s dinosaur bones and other fossils were found in the clay pits. Many of these fossils are now at the Smithsonian. At the time, many more spectacular dinosaur fossil sites were being found in the American West, which became the focus of most fossil collecting. During the first half of the twentieth century, fossils were still collected, but much of the collecting activity had nearly ceased until the early 1990s. Additional dinosaur bones were found, and in 1995 Prince George's County acquired 22 acres of the former pits. This later became Dinosaur Park, which opened in 2009.

Dinosaur Park is open to the public the first and third Saturday of every month from noon to 4 p.m., and is otherwise closed and inaccessible. It is one of the few sites in the Washington area that is free, which is a huge plus if you come to the site with your family. We visited the site in July 2014. They have several volunteers, and Prince George's County actually has a paleontologist on staff at the park. Fossil collecting at the park is limited to looking for bones, teeth, and fossil pinecones on the surface of the former pits. Detailed studies of the site indicate that the pollen and spores in the clay pit are ferns, seed

Lignite is abundant at the park, and you are allowed to collect small pieces.

ferns, shrubby conifers, cypress-type conifers, and tree-size conifers. The site is interpreted as a wetland that was developed on the clay floor of a waning oxbow lake. It is also known for the bones of *Astrodon*, which is a large plant-eating dinosaur that is also the Maryland state dinosaur.

While the surface is constantly picked over by collectors, every time it rains more fossils are exposed. The fossils are nearly the same color as the siderite and limonite, and it takes a sharp eye to pick them out. The clay pits are also full of lignite, which is a carbonized wood. You can keep small pieces of lignite, but the park requests that any other fossils that you find be provided to the museum for their records. The park staff and volunteers at the site do an excellent job with their presentations and help with collecting, and Prince George's County has made the right decision in opening the park for limiting collecting and keeping it free. It is well worth a visit, especially if you can come after a major rainstorm.

References: Bernstein, 1979; Kranz, 1989; Robbins, 1991

65. Bladensburg Siderite and Limonite

The hillside at this site is barren and has reddish-orange soils, and nodules of siderite and limonite can be easily found along the slopes.

See map page 221.
County: Prince George's
Site type: Eroded hillside
Land status: Uncertain, not posted but some areas fenced
Material: Siderite and limonite nodules
Host rock: Atlantic Coastal Plain sediments of the Cretaceous Patapsco Formation
Difficulty: Moderate
Family-friendly: No; hillside is very steep
Tools needed: Hammer and gloves
Special concerns: Land access questionable, lots of trash, industrial area
Special attractions: Washington, DC
GPS parking: 38°55'57"N / 76°55'33"W

Topographic quadrangle: Washington East, DC–MD

Finding the site: Head south on MD 295 and take the exit for MD 202 North. Go 0.4 mile and turn left (south) onto 55th Avenue. Go 0.1 mile and turn right (west) onto Newton Street. Go 0.3 mile and turn left (south) onto 52nd Avenue. Go 0.2 mile and turn left (east) onto Lawrence Place. Go 0.3 mile and park on the side of the road. The outcrops are on the hill just to the south of Lawrence Place.

Rockhounding

This fine-grained limonitic siltstone has orange and purple bands.

This is an urban site that offers the opportunity to find siderite and limonite nodules. The area is a large hillside with an exposure of Atlantic Coastal Plain sediments that are mainly of the Cretaceous Patapsco Formation. Silicified wood and marcasite in lignitized wood are also reported from this area.

However, this site is not for the squeamish. We stopped here on our way back from the Smithsonian in Washington, DC, and arrived early Saturday evening while it was still light. The area is surrounded by industrial buildings that appear to be circa 1970s–1980s, and the steady beat of Latin and rap music from the nightclubs that were opening was already reverberating throughout area. We parked our car next to the hillside, and my wife and daughter were immediately disgusted by the site garbage, which included a diaper that was hanging on the fence near the entry point to climb up the hillside. As an experienced urban collector, I am not bothered by trash, but make certain to avoid broken glass, nails in boards, and stepping in puddles. The land was not posted, and there were indications that lots of people enter the area. Based on information from Google Maps, it appears to be within lands of the Maryland Department of Transportation, as the site is adjacent to MD 295, which is also known as the Baltimore-Washington Parkway.

The hillside gets very steep, but you can pull yourself upwards by grabbing onto exposed roots and cutting steps for your feet in the clay with your hammer. It is relatively easy to find colorful red to brown siderite nodules, and breaking them open often reveals multicolored bands that range from light orange to bright red. I did not find any silicified wood, marcasite, or lignite, but my time was limited due to the lack of remaining daylight. Climbing down the hillside was also an adventure, and poison ivy is another potential hazard at this site, as the lower slopes are overgrown with vegetation. As the area is an industrial park and undoubtedly gets a lot of traffic during the day, I recommend visiting this site after work hours or on a weekend to ensure that you do not disrupt the nearby businesses or otherwise call attention to yourself.

References: Cleaves et al., 1968; Bernstein, 1980

Sites 64–65

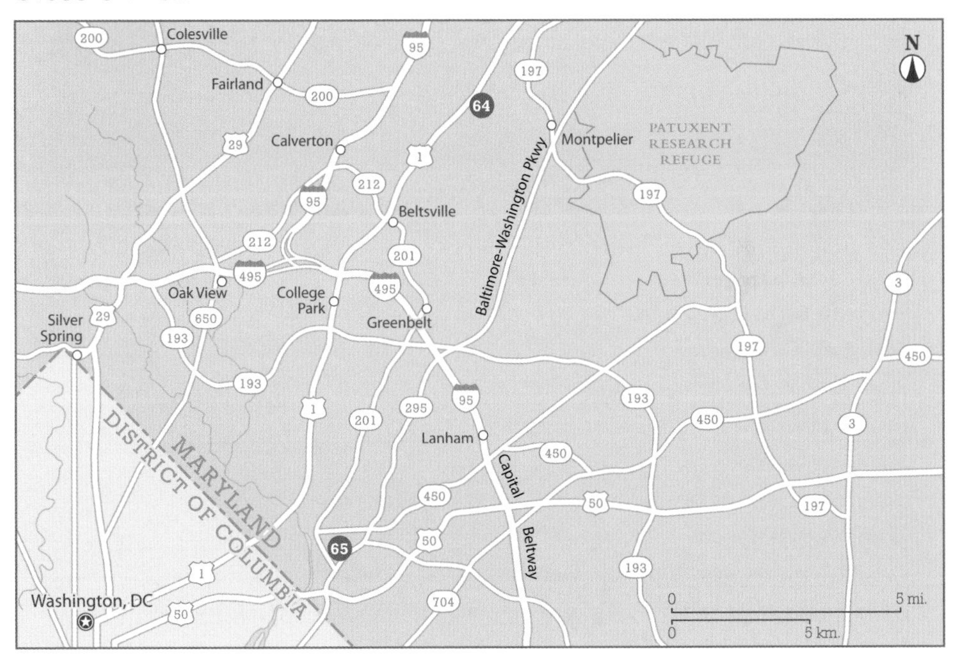

66. Wheeler Road Vivianite

Vivianite can be found on this broad exposure along Wheeler Road.

See map page 227.
County: Prince George's
Site type: Multitiered roadcut
Land status: Private, upper tier posted
Material: Vivianite
Host rock: Green-gray clay beneath clayey sand and gravel
Difficulty: Moderate
Family-friendly: No; upper tier woods posted, lots of trash on roadside
Tools needed: Hammer with pick end to dig loose rocks from mud
Special concerns: Posted land, site trash
Special attractions: Washington, DC
GPS parking: 38°49'48"N / 76°58'55"W
Topographic quadrangle: Anacostia, DC–MD

Finding the site: From I-95 South, take exit 4B for MD 414. Go 0.3 mile, keep right at the fork, and merge onto MD 414 East. Go 0.4 mile and turn left (northwest) onto Wheeler Road. Go 1.5 miles, and you will see a long, broad outcrop on the hillside on the northeast side of Wheeler Road. Park at a safe place along the shoulder and walk to the outcrop.

Rockhounding

This small piece of vivianite was found on the hillside in a small gully.

This used to be an excellent locality for vivianite, but as of June 2014 the woods above the upper zone are posted against trespassing. I had never seen posted signs at this site during previous trips, and this particular sign was among the most threatening I have encountered. It was on a tree in the woods and was a bright yellow, no trespassing sign with the owner listed as Prince George's Police, with YOU WILL BE ARRESTED in capital letters in the space normally reserved for contact information. The outcrop itself is outside of the posted zone, but I have no desire to have any contact whatsoever with the Prince George's Police, so my last visit to this site was limited to what loose rocks I could observe along the outcrop from the roadside.

During my previous trips to this site, vivianite nodules were abundant. Vivianite is a hydrous iron phosphate, and the formula is $Fe_3(PO_4)_2 8H_2O$. The blue of vivianite is often described as "Prussian blue." The nodules are found directly beneath the unconformable contact of the Upper Cretaceous Severn Formation and the overlying Miocene Calvert Formation. The zone with the nodules is limonite-rich sandy clay with sand and gravel, and is reportedly fossiliferous. The nodules are like small geodes, and the vivianite often forms in the nodules as blue prismatic crystals.

Artists have long experimented with vivianite as a pigment for blue paint. Vivianite has a hardness of only 1.5-2, so it was easily crushed and produced a beautiful blue. Unfortunately, as a hydrous iron phosphate, vivianite is unstable. It does not like light, and the blue crystals will darken to black and may even disintegrate. This is caused by the partial oxidation of ferrous to ferric iron on exposure to light. With further oxidation, the crystals turn to brownish hydrous iron oxides. This made it a terrible pigment.

In the days before modern paints, the main pigments for blue were almost entirely limited to lazurite, azurite, or vivianite. Nearly all the lazurite came from Afghanistan and was extremely expensive. Azurite was common, but upon exposure to dampness and carbon dioxide, it would often convert to green malachite. Vivianite would turn dark, so it was the worst option. Fortunately the advent of chemistry and industrial processes soon produced economical pigments for Prussian blue, and artists no longer have to rely on expensive and fickle natural minerals for blue paint. Early visitors to this locality may have also crushed the deep blue nodules and painted with the powder, but they were undoubtedly soon disappointed with the results.

Due to the threatening nature of the posted sign, I did not get to spend much time looking for vivianite at this site. My family was with me at the time, and they were also turned off by the extensive amount of broken bottles and garbage along the roadside. The outcrop is highly weathered, and loose rocks from the upper tier are constantly washing into the small drainage ditch next to the road. I found several pieces of limonite on the roadside, and luckily found a small blue nodule that had washed down a small gully on the outcrop. This was a rounded piece that I cracked open, and it had radiating blue crystals. In the past I could easily find many similar pieces at this site. Visiting the site after a rainstorm may pay off, as the vivianite will wash down from the nodular-bearing zone, and you can access this zone without encroaching on the posted areas.

The exposed blue crystals of the nodule that I found have already oxidized to dark brown, so I will have to return again if I want blue vivianite crystals. However, if you go to this site, be aware that it may be watched by the police, and even if you are well outside of the posted areas, you may attract unwanted attention. A hefty fine to a rockhound may be viewed as an excellent way to increase revenues.

References: Beard, 2004; Bernstein, 1980

67. Henson Creek Tributary Fossils

The stream banks are almost entirely made of fossils at this site.

See map page 227.
County: Prince George's
Site type: Stream outcrop and loose fossils in stream
Land status: Uncertain, not posted
Material: Mollusks and *Turritella* fossils
Host rock: Greensand of Paleocene Lower Aquia Formation
Difficulty: Easy
Family-friendly: Yes
Tools needed: Hammer
Special concerns: Land status, parking, fossils in outcrop are very soft
Special attractions: Washington, DC
GPS parking: 38°48'14"N / 76°57'10"W
GPS stream bed: 38°48'16"N / 76°57'33"W

Topographic quadrangle: Anacostia, DC–MD
Finding the site: From I-95 South, take exit 4A to merge onto MD 414 West. Go 0.6 mile and turn left (south) onto St. Barnabas Road, then quickly turn left (east) onto Brinkley Road. In 0.8 mile you will cross a small bridge, which is just before the intersection. Continue another 0.4 mile to the small parking lot for the Rosecroft Shopping Center. Park here and walk west back to the creek that you just crossed. The fossils are found on the creek just south of this bridge.

Rockhounding

Large fossils that weathered from the banks can be found downstream of the fossiliferous outcrop.

The first time I came to this site, I was shocked when I saw the rocks exposed on the stream bank. The banks are nearly entirely made of fossils, and you can see the outlines of bivalves and the tightly coiled pattern of *Turritella* shells. These rocks are fossiliferous sections of the Paleocene Aquia Formation, which is dark green to gray-green argillaceous sand. The banks, however, are extremely soft, and trying to pull fossils out of the banks was futile, as they would immediately disintegrate. I found it was much more productive to look at the loose rocks in the streambed. Many of the larger dark gray rocks were large bivalves.

This site is known for the presence of *Cucullaea*, which is a large extinct clam that can be nearly 6 inches in length. Very large *Ostrea* oysters also occur at this site. The fossil-bearing outcrops are confined to an area that begins approximately 100 feet south of the bridge and continues for another 200 feet or so. The exposures are then covered by alluvium.

Most of the fossiliferous rocks in the stream are found near the banks with exposed fossils. This is likely because the fossils are very soft and cannot wash farther downstream without being completely destroyed. The streambed is also made of rounded rocks of quartz, sandstone, and other hard rocks. Some of these fit the definition of "Potomac agate," which is not really an agate at all but simply weathered and rounded silica-rich rock. If you go to this site, make sure that you do not overcollect the fossils, as localities like this are relatively small and it is easy to remove too may rocks.

Reference: Glaser, 1979

Sites 66–69

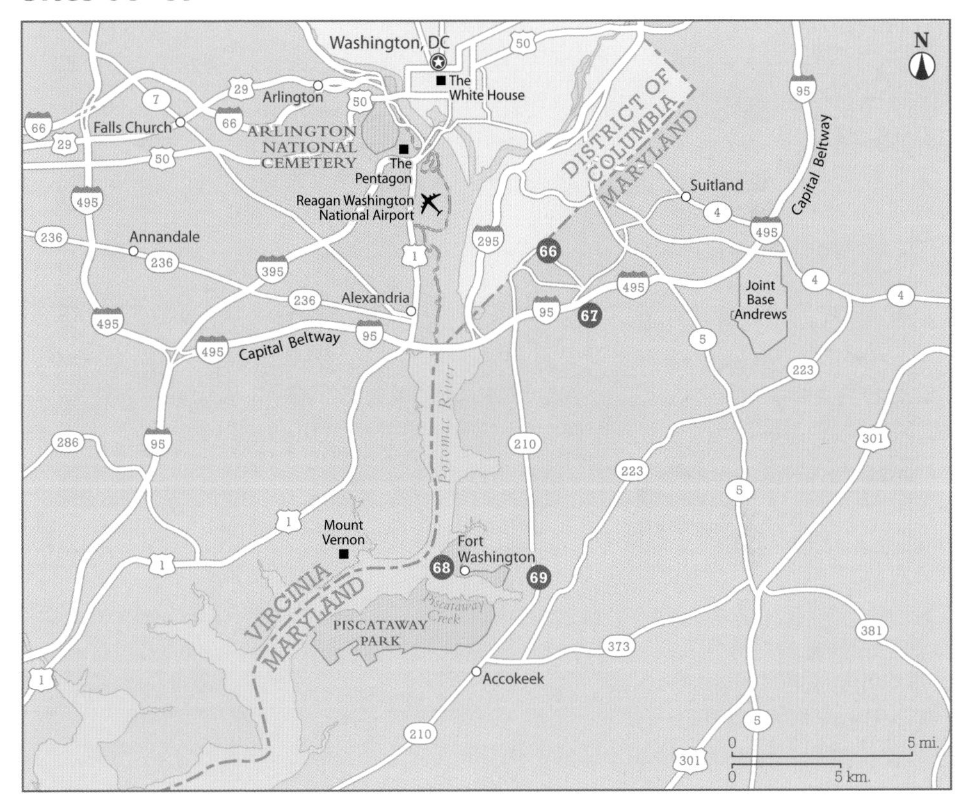

68. Fort Washington Gypsum Crystals and Fulgarites

The cliffs are steep, and the gypsum crystals are found in the slumping clays and the exposed cliff sides.

See map page 227.
County: Prince George's
Site type: Eroding cliffs
Land status: Fort Washington National Park
Material: Gypsum crystals and fulgarites
Host rock: Clays in Cretaceous Monmouth Formation
Difficulty: Easy
Family-friendly: Yes
Tools needed: None
Special concerns: National park; no collecting allowed
Special attractions: Fort Washington National Park ruins and scenic views
GPS parking: 38°42'31"N / 77°01'34"W

GPS clay outcrops: 38°42'13"N / 77°01'48"W
Topographic quadrangle: Mount Vernon, VA–MD
Finding the site: From I-95 South, take exit 3 towards Indian Head. Merge onto MD 210, go 4.4 miles, and turn right onto Fort Washington Road. Go 1.7 miles and at the traffic circle, continue straight to stay on Fort Washington Road. Continue on Fort Washington Road, and after the road makes a broad turn to the right (west), you will enter Fort Washington National Park. This is approximately 1.7 miles after the traffic circle. Take the first left (south), go approximately 0.3 mile, and park in the southernmost parking area. Walk south, and the road towards the woods soon ends and becomes a trail towards the river. Hike on this trail to the cliffs. You will pass some large concrete ruins to the right as you near the cliffs. The trail to the base of the cliffs is steep but not difficult. The gypsum is in the dark black clay that has slumped from the cliffs, and can also be found in the tan sediments on the cliff face.

Rockhounding

Fort Washington, originally called Fort Warburton, was built in 1809 to defend the US capital. In August 1814, with British forces in Washington and British ships coming up the Potomac River, the fort was destroyed by its own troops to prevent its capture and use by the enemy. After the war the fort was eventually rebuilt and equipped with more concrete batteries and large guns, and was used for the defense of Washington during the Civil War. During World War I the fort was used for staging troops, and during World War II it was used as an army training school. In 1946 the fort was transferred to the Department of the Interior and has since been a park operated by the National

Radiating gypsum crystals can be found on the surface and within the dark gray clay at the cliffs.

Park Service. It is a very accessible park and offers a welcome respite from the traffic and congestion of Washington, DC.

This is a fulgarite, which formed by the fusing of sediments from lightning striking the cliff.

In addition to the park history, this is one of the most interesting and scenic geologic sites in the DC area. The cliffs are Cretaceous clays and siltstones of the Monmouth Formation. When I first visited the site on a late Sunday afternoon in June 2014, I knew I was heading in the right direction when I heard voices on the beach below the cliffs. Another group was looking at gypsum crystals at the base of the cliffs, and I got some excellent guidance on where to see the crystals. The best place to find the biggest gypsum crystals is in the large mass of dark gray clay that has slumped off the cliffs. Washing some of the finds with water often revealed radiating gypsum crystals, and many had a "starburst" pattern emanating from a roughly flat base. Many of the other crystals were simply flat, elongated blades. The crystals are composed of clear selenite gypsum, but the fine dark clays have permeated the finely laminated plates of the crystals, and the clays are impossible to completely wash away. This results in dark gray crystals that appear to be coated with mud, but the radiating pattern more than makes up for the lack of transparency. Some lighter-colored gypsum crystals can also be seen in the cliff outcrops, and since these are not in the dark clay, they tend to be more transparent.

The leader of the group also showed me something I had never seen before in Maryland. The beach is full of other interesting rocks, including some fossil casts, and while looking at these rocks he picked up a dense, iron-rich rock that appeared to be an oddly shaped conglomerate. He said that this was a fulgarite, which formed from lightning striking the cliffs and fusing sediments together. Fulgarites are not uncommon, but a place where you can find so many on the beach is unique. The cliffs are positioned perfectly to bear the brunt of lightning storms that come from the southeast, so it is not surprising to see fulgarites at this site.

The site offers an incredible view of the Potomac River and mouth of Piscataway Creek, and after you visit the cliffs, it is worthwhile to explore the rest of the park. While this is a national park and collecting is not allowed, it still offers a unique opportunity to see gypsum crystals in their host clays and fulgarites on the beach. If you go during the summer, be sure to bring a hat, sunscreen, and lots of drinking water, as the southwest-facing cliffs expose you to the full force of the afternoon sun.

References: Cleaves, 1968; Bernstein, 1980

69. Piscataway Creek Tributary *Turritella* and Armored Mud Balls

The outcrops exposed in the stream at this location are full of *Turritella* fossils.

See map page 227.
County: Prince George's
Site type: Outcrops and loose rocks in creek
Land status: Piscataway Creek Stream Valley Park
Material: *Turritella* fossil shells and armored mud balls
Host rock: Miocene Nanjemoy Formation, Late Paleocene–Early Eocene Marlboro clay
Difficulty: Moderate
Family-friendly: Only for the most adventurous families
Tools needed: Hammer, gloves

Special concerns: Heavy overgrowth, traffic along MD 210, collecting status uncertain
Special attractions: Fort Washington National Park
GPS parking: 38°41'58"N / 76°59'11"W
GPS fossil outcrops: 38°42'09"N / 76°59'13"W
Topographic quadrangle: Piscataway, MD
Finding the site: The only way I know to access this site is from MD 210 North. From I-95, take exit 3 toward Indian Head and merge onto MD 210 South. Continue south on MD 210 for approximately 8 miles. After you cross the bridge over Piscataway Creek, take the next exit and return north on MD 210. Cross the bridge and pull over into a broad area on the shoulder. This is a reasonably safe place to park, as it is well off the road. Look for a trail that enters the woods, and follow this down to a tributary that flows into Piscataway Creek. Hike up the tributary, parallel to MD 210, for approximately 1,000 feet to the fossiliferous outcrops.

Rockhounding

This is an excellent locality to see an outcrop comprised almost entirely of *Turritella* fossils and an interesting occurrence of armored mud balls, which I had never seen before in the field. The *Turritella* fossils occur in dark gray sandy clay of the Nanjemoy Formation, and the armored mud balls formed from clays that may have eroded from the underlying Marlboro clay.

The armored mud balls may represent pieces of Marlboro clay that broke free and tumbled down the streambed.

We had a terrible time finding this site, as we first looked for other places to park besides MD 210. Just before we were about to quit, we found that we could park just north of the Piscataway Creek bridge on the east side of northbound MD 210. My daughter and I climbed down to the tributary, and it was full of granitic and metamorphic stream rocks but no fossils. She soon went back to the car to join her mother and brother, as she did not want to get her shoes muddy. While everyone else waited in the car, I hiked up the tributary. I thought it would only take a few minutes to find the outcrop. I kept hiking and hiking up the tributary, which soon became overgrown with vegetation and often blocked by fallen trees. I did not see any fossils, but noticed very strange round, red masses of clay that were studded with rocks. These were armored mud balls, which apparently formed from broken masses of Marlboro clay. They formed a nucleus to collect loose rocks as they rolled down the creek bed, picking up rocks like a snowball.

This *Turritella* shell is nearly intact but is very fragile.

I was about to give up, but decided to make one last push upstream. I noticed that the steep banks suddenly transitioned to a flat area, and I saw a loose rock with a *Turritella* fragment in the streambed. I knew that I was close at that point. About 100 feet up the stream, I found that the ravine became extremely narrow, and the bank outcrops were dark gray clays that were practically all *Turritella* fossils. I was able to find some loose pieces in the stream, and some of the fossils in the outcrop could be extracted without breaking them. Unfortunately by this time I had to get back to the car, and the remaining daylight was limited.

This locality also reportedly has shark teeth that weather from the overlying Calvert Formation, but I did not see any teeth and did not get to see the Calvert Formation. The ravine near the *Turritella* outcrops gets very narrow in this area and is also full of large blocks of concrete that were apparently dumped from a construction project. The fossils in the Nanjemoy Formation alone are well worth the trip, and getting to see the armored mud balls is an added bonus.

References: Bell, 1940; Glaser, 1979

70. Purse State Park Shark Teeth and *Turritella* Fossils

The shoreline at Purse State Park has a shark tooth–rich beach and outcrops of fossiliferous rocks.

County: Charles
Site type: Beach and outcrops
Land status: Purse State Park
Material: Shark teeth and *Turritella* fossils
Host rock: Beach sands and Paleocene Aquia Formation
Difficulty: Easy
Family-friendly: Yes
Tools needed: None; collecting not allowed
Special concerns: Moderate hike to site, relatively remote
Special attractions: None
GPS parking: 38°25'56"N / 77°15'06"W
GPS beach: 38°25'55"N / 77°15'23"W

GPS fossil outcrops: 38°25'23"N / 77°15'41"W
Topographic quadrangle: Widewater, VA–MD
Finding the site: From I-95 South, take exit 3 towards Indian Head and continue on MD 210 South for 18.1 miles. Turn left onto MD 225 East, go 1.6 miles, and turn right onto MD 224 South. Continue 15.1 miles south on MD 224 and look for a parking area on the left (east) side of the road. Park here and follow the trail to the beach. Shark teeth can be found on the beach, and fossils are present where outcrops occur. The largest and most fossiliferous outcrops can be reached by walking south on the beach to the first major point.

Rockhounding

This is a favorite beach of many shark teeth collectors, and it is also one of my favorites, as it has both abundant shark teeth and an amazing concentration of fossils in outcrops and loose rocks. We brought a shovel and a screen, but found that the best way to find shark teeth is to walk along the beach and watch the shifting sands as the waves lap onto the beach. In about an hour my daughter found nearly a handful of shark teeth. Many of the teeth that she found were extremely narrow with sharp points, and these are reportedly from *Scapanorhynchus*, which is an extinct genus of shark that is similar to the living goblin shark.

Many of these teeth appear to be from *Scapanorhynchus*, which was related to the goblin shark.

When you reach the beach by the trail, you will notice that some small cliffs are present just north of the trail. Fossils are abundant in the rocks exposed in this area, and many of these are *Turritella*, which are tightly coiled sea snails that are shaped like a narrow cone. Most of the fossils are very weathered and crumble when touched, but some of their casts are intact. Some of the interiors of the *Turritella* are

These *Turritella* casts were found in an outcrop near the trail that leads to the beach.

preserved by fine mud that has filled their interior spaces and has remained intact long after the original shells have eroded away. These casts are like a negative image of the original animal's shell.

If you can, walk south along the beach to the small point on the river. This is just south of a swampy area that drains into the river. This area has huge outcrops of the Aquia Formation, and virtually the entire rock is made of fossils. The outcrops have *Turritella* and bivalves, and many of them are very hard and are found as loose pieces next to the outcrops and the large boulders that have fallen onto the shoreline.

This is a fairly remote area, and many people that visit the beach come here by boat, not via the trail. Depending on your timing you may be the only visitor, especially if you come in the off-season. If you are able to visit during low tide, you will likely be one of the first beach walkers of the day, and this is the best time to find shark teeth on the beach.

Reference: Glaser, 1979

Sites 70–73

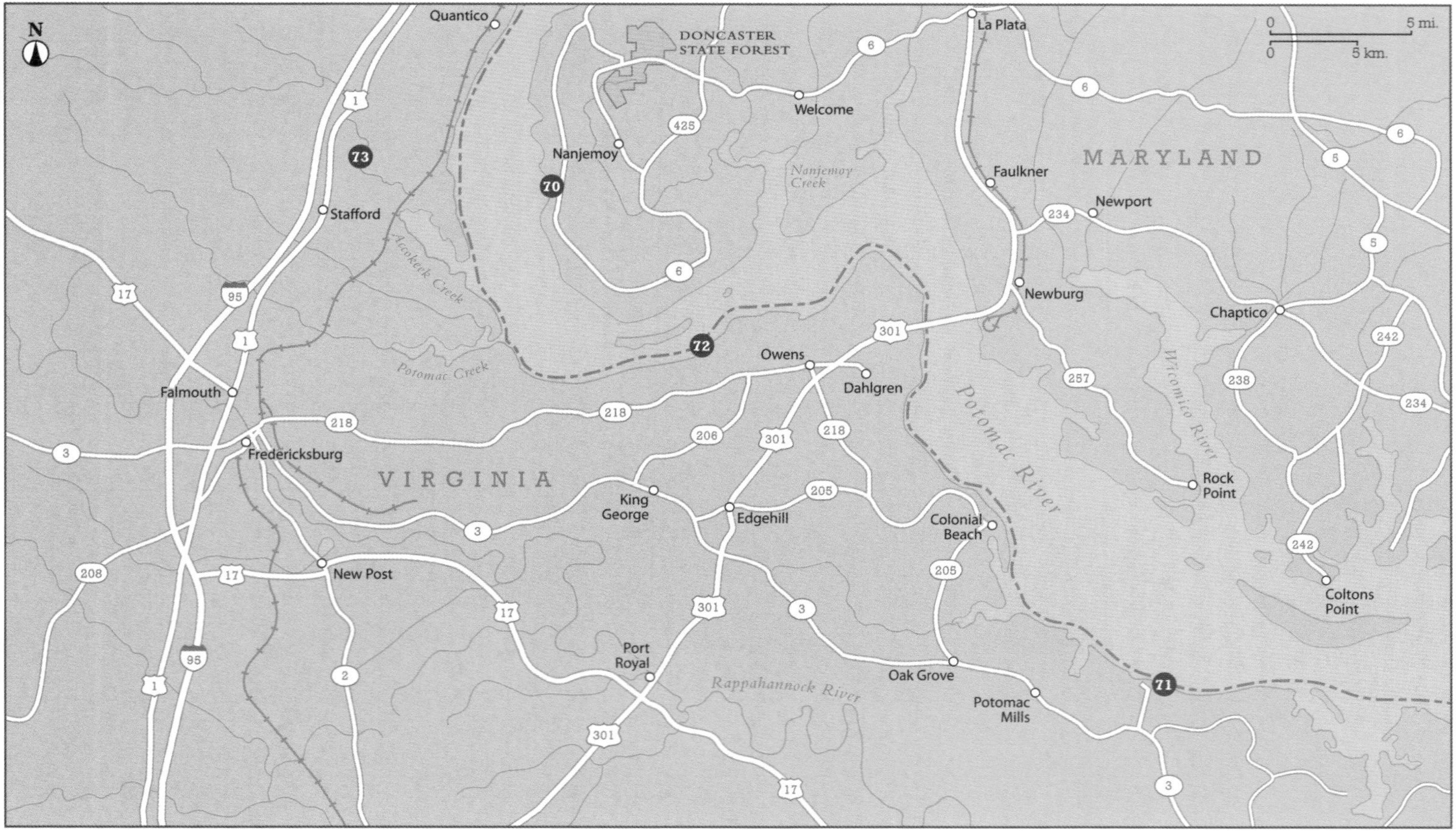

N
0 5 mi.
0 5 km.
MARYLAND
VIRGINIA
DONCASTER STATE FOREST
Quantico
La Plata
Welcome
Nanjemoy
Nanjemoy Creek
Faulkner
Newport
Newburg
Chaptico
Stafford
Accokeek Creek
Potomac Creek
Falmouth
Fredericksburg
Owens
Dahlgren
Potomac River
Wicomico River
Rock Point
King George
Edgehill
Colonial Beach
New Post
Port Royal
Rappahannock River
Oak Grove
Potomac Mills
Coltons Point
70
71
72
73

71. Westmoreland State Park Shark Teeth

Westmoreland State Park beach is next to large cliffs that constantly erode and drop more shark teeth into the surf.

See map page 238.

County: Westmoreland, VA
Site type: Beach
Land status: Westmoreland State Park
Material: Shark teeth
Host rock: Beach sediments, weathered from Miocene Choptank Formation
Difficulty: Easy to moderate
Family-friendly: Yes
Tools needed: None; digging prohibited
Special concerns: Must stay away from cliffs
Special attractions: Impressive shark teeth display at visitor center
GPS parking: 38°10'11"N / 76°51'49"W

GPS Fossil Beach: 38°10'01"N / 76°51'16"W
Topographic quadrangle: Stratford Hall, VA–MD
Finding the site: From US 301, turn left onto VA 3 East. Go 17.7 miles and turn left onto VA 347 North to enter Westmoreland State Park. Go 1.8 miles and turn right onto VA 686. Go 0.2 mile and park at the visitor center parking lot. From here you can hike a little over 0.5 mile on the Big Meadow Trail to the aptly named Fossil Beach, which is the main beach for hikers to collect shark teeth in the park.

Rockhounding

This is a well-known beach for shark teeth in Virginia. The shark teeth are from extinct Miocene sharks and from sediments of the Choptank Formation of the Chesapeake Group. The visitor center has a great display of shark teeth, but it is important to remember that these were collected over decades and long before the beach was the focus of shark teeth collecting.

This display of shark teeth in the visitor center gives you a sense of what has been found at Westmoreland State Park, especially in the early years of collecting at the beach.

We arrived on a rainy June morning, so we did not have a lot of competition from other collectors. We were among the first people on the beach, but more showed up as the weather began to improve slightly. We first used a small screen to sift through the sand and gravel of the shoreline, but soon focused on just looking for teeth at the water's edge without a screen. We were only able to find small teeth, but a young boy found a large tooth that appeared to be from a goblin shark, and a lady with her family found a very large tooth just walking along the beach. The teeth are there, but it takes patience and luck to find them. Some parts of Westmoreland State Park are also only accessible by boat, and these areas are also frequented by shark teeth hunters, but for now our collecting is limited to where we can reach by hiking.

References: Ward and Blackwelder, 1980; Frye, 1986

This large tooth was picked up on the beach and was one of the largest teeth that we saw at this beach.

72. Caledon State Park Shark Teeth

Watching the waves wash teeth onto the beach still seems the best way to find shark teeth.

See map page 238.
County: King George, VA
Site type: Beach
Land status: Caledon State Park
Material: Shark teeth
Host rock: Beach sediments
Difficulty: Easy
Family-friendly: Yes
Tools needed: None, but a small shovel/screen may be useful
Special concerns: Moderate hike to beach
Special attractions: Solitude, fishing on Potomac River
GPS parking: 38°20'02"N / 77°08'35"W
GPS beach: 38°20'55"N / 77°09'28"W

Topographic quadrangle: King George, VA–MD
Finding the site: From I-95, take exit 133A and merge onto US 17 South. Go 2.1 miles, and this turns into VA 218 East. Follow this for 20.2 miles, then make a slight left (north) onto the road for the park. Continue to the right for 0.2 mile and park in the parking lot near the buildings. The trailhead for the Boyd's Hole Trail, which goes to the beach, is directly to the north. On the way to the beach, you will encounter an area known as the Triangle. Stay on the Boyd's Hole Trail, which is the right fork at the Triangle, and you will soon reach the beach. The total hike is approximately 1.25 miles.

Rockhounding

This is a very long and secluded beach that has large shark teeth. We came to the site as the tide was coming in, and we were able to find several teeth by walking along the shore and simply looking down where the waves met the shoreline. Some of these were much larger than we had found at Westmoreland Beach, Virginia, and nearby Purse State Park in Maryland. The beach area does not have any significant cliffs. We attempted to walk to some small cliffs upstream and to the west, but were soon stopped by both the cliffs and signs stating we would be entering private land. The beach is loaded with driftwood, but fortunately most of this wood is away from the shore so it is easy to walk along the shoreline without climbing or tripping over logs. While collecting shark teeth is allowed, driftwood collecting is not.

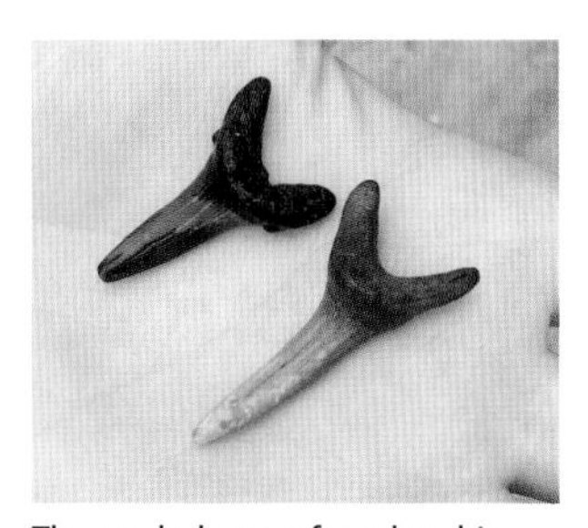
The teeth that we found at this beach were much larger than those at many other beaches.

Reference: Virginia Department of Mineral Resources, 2003

73. Government Island Sandstone Quarry

The cuts made to carve the sandstone nearly 200 years ago are still prominent on the sandstone.

See map page 238.

County: Stafford, VA
Site type: Former sandstone quarry
Land status: Stafford County Parks and Recreation
Material: Brown sandstone
Host rock: Cretaceous Aquia Creek Formation
Difficulty: Easy
Family-friendly: Yes
Tools needed: None
Special concerns: County park; no collecting allowed, strictly for observation only
Special attractions: Several local Civil War sites
GPS parking: 38°26'48.9"N / 77°23'18"W

GPS quarry area: 38°26'59"N / 77°22'48"W
Topographic quadrangle: Stafford, VA
Finding the site: From I-95 North, take exit 140 for CR 630. Go 0.2 mile and turn right (east) onto Courthouse Road. Go 0.7 mile and turn left (north) onto US 1 North. Go 1.7 miles and turn right (east) onto Coal Landing Road. Go 0.7 mile and look for the parking area to your left (north). From here you can follow the trail to Government Island and the former quarry. The address for the parking area is 191 Coal Landing Rd., Stafford, VA 22554.

Rockhounding

Government Island is a former quarry that supplied stone for many buildings in Washington, DC, and the surrounding region. The land for the quarry was bought in 1791 to supply stone for the nation's new capital in Washington. The quarry was positioned next to the Potomac River, and the stone was loaded on barges and transported to the capital. Washington was still nearly 50 miles away and upstream, so it must have been quite a task to get the stone to

The main quarry area is watched by a security camera.

the capital. The buildings that incorporated the stone into their construction include the White House, the US Capitol, and the US Treasury.

The Cretaceous Aquia Creek sandstone is known as "freestone," as it is a fine-grained stone that can be easily cut in any direction without splitting. However, it was a terrible building stone. Despite the relatively consistent grain size, the stone had lumps of clay and occasional large pebbles, and some sections were poorly cemented. By the early 1800s the limitations of the stone were obvious, and the last use of it for buildings was in 1827. In 1849 the head of the building committee for the Smithsonian Institution said that he would not want the stone even if it were free. The quarry soon fell into disuse and was abandoned.

In the late twentieth century, the historic significance of the site was recognized, and in 2009 the former quarry was established as a county park with trails and interpretative signs. The quarry has a trail that circles Government Island, and from the parking lot it is a 1.5-mile walk. The area is also an ideal location to see plants, birds, and wildlife, and many people also fish in Aquia Creek in the park. The quarry was also featured on the History Channel on November 9, 2013, in *10 Things You Don't Know About: The White House.* I caught this show just by chance and made a promise to myself to find and visit this quarry.

The Cretaceous Aquia Creek sandstone should not be confused with the Paleocene Aquia Formation, as the Aquia Formation is very soft since it is made of glauconitic sand and clay. When we visited the area, we were able to walk around the entire island and visit some of the former quarried areas. The Aquia Creek sandstone is consistently brown and fine-to-medium grained, and you can see some of the differential weathering that ultimately made it a poor stone for building material. The county is apparently very serious about no collecting at this site, as a security camera is positioned in the main quarry area. This is the part of the island that almost certainly gets the most visitors. Assuming it is a motion-activated camera, it must be a real challenge to manage all of the resulting image and video data for this quarry.

References: *Free Lance Star*, 1992; USGS, 1998

74. Leesburg Potomac Marble

The outcrops of Potomac marble form prominent knobs on the hillside.

County: Loudoun, VA
Site type: Outcrops
Land status: Ida Lee Park
Material: Potomac marble
Host rock: Triassic Leesburg member of the Balls Bluff siltstone
Difficulty: Easy
Family-friendly: Yes
Tools needed: None, collecting not allowed
Special concerns: None
Special attractions: Morven Park Estate, Ball's Bluff Battlefield and National Cemetery
GPS parking: 39°07'28"N / 77°34'05"W
GPS outcrops: 39°07'36"N / 77°34'07"W

Topographic quadrangle: Waterford, VA–MD

Finding the site: Take US 15 South towards Leesburg. Stay to the right to get on US 15 Business South, continue 1.3 miles, and turn right (west) onto Ida Lee Drive NW. Continue 0.3 mile, then turn left (southwest) onto an unnamed road, go 0.1 mile, and turn left (southwest) into a parking lot. Park here and walk to the park.

Rockhounding

This group of outcrops at Ida Lee Park is often the site of geologic field trips, as the rocks are well exposed and there is parking for groups. Potomac marble is formally known as the Leesburg limestone conglomeratic member of the Bull Run Formation, and is Triassic in age. The Leesburg member is a distinct carbonate conglomerate with subangular to subrounded pebbles, cobbles, and boulders of limestone and dolomite in a reddish-brown silty matrix. The carbonate clasts are likely from the Cambrian–early Paleozoic Frederick Limestone and Tomstown Formations, which are exposed in the region of Furnace Mountain and north of the Potomac River in Frederick

The rock is extremely hard to break, but the variability of the stone clasts makes it hard to use as building stone.

County, Maryland. The conglomerate is interpreted to be from debris flows on alluvial fans.

Potomac marble, also known as calico rock or Potomac breccia, was quarried and used for the columns in Statuary Hall in the Capitol in Washington, DC. While the stone has a beautiful pattern, it has many other features that make it a terrible building stone. It has considerable variety in texture, clasts can fall out, and when used outside, it is subjected to differential weathering of the limestone, dolomite, and matrix.

The outcrops are exposed on the hillside in grassy areas, and it is possible to walk directly to the rocks to see the outcrops. The outcrops that I saw were very hard and solid, and I did not see any large pieces of float, which are loose pieces of rock lying around outcrops. The area is regularly mowed and any float could cause damage to the mower, so it likely has long been removed. The outcrops form prominent knobs on the surface, and it is easy to see why early quarrymen mined the stone and cut it into large blocks for buildings. It is ironic that the very qualities that make it attractive, namely the variable white to gray clasts in a red matrix, also make it a poor choice for long-term exterior stone. Rocks of carbonate clasts in a silty matrix are doomed to fail much sooner than most other building stones.

References: Smoot, 1989; Southworth et al., 1999

Sites 74–78

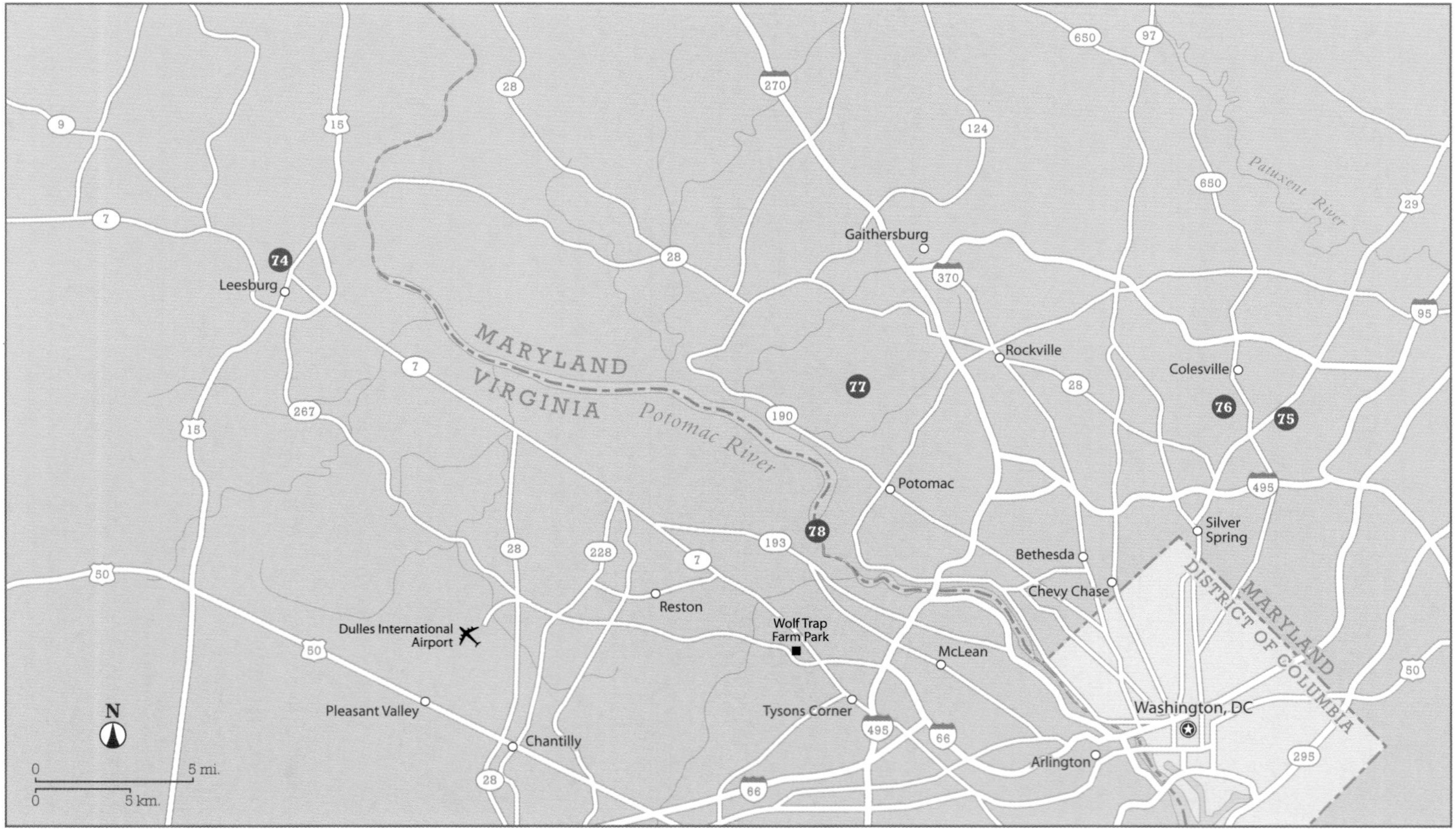

Leesburg
Gaithersburg
Rockville
Colesville
Potomac
Silver Spring
Bethesda
Chevy Chase
Reston
Wolf Trap Farm Park
McLean
Dulles International Airport
Pleasant Valley
Chantilly
Tysons Corner
Arlington
Washington, DC
MARYLAND
VIRGINIA
MARYLAND
DISTRICT OF COLUMBIA
Potomac River
Patuxent River
74
75
76
77
78
N
0 5 mi.
0 5 km.

75. Paint Branch Orange Feldspar and Micaceous Gneiss

Feldspar and mica are easily found at the stream bends of Paint Branch.

See map page 250.

County: Montgomery
Site type: Loose rocks and outcrops in stream and hillside
Land status: Montgomery County Department of Parks
Material: Orange feldspar and micaceous gneissic schist
Host rock: Boulder gneiss of the Glenarm series
Difficulty: Easy
Family-friendly: Yes
Tools needed: Hammer
Special concerns: Limited parking
Special attractions: Washington, DC
GPS parking: 39°02'59"N / 76°58'45"W

GPS stream bend with abundant rocks: 39°02'59"N / 76°58'45"W
GPS micaceous gneiss boulder area: 39°02'59"N / 76°58'45"W
Topographic quadrangle: Beltsville, MD
Finding the site: This can be a tricky site to find. Old Columbia Pike, which is the road on which to park, has been closed east of the bridge over Paint Branch, and you should make sure that your GPS does not tell you to approach the site from the east. To get to the site, head west on I-495 West, then take exit 28A and merge onto MD 650 North. Go 2 miles and merge onto US 29 North. Go 0.4 mile and turn right onto Stewart Lane. Take the next left immediately onto Old Columbia Pike and continue 0.5 mile to where the road is blocked off. Park here on the side of the road and walk to the bridge. A trail leading down to Paint Branch is on the east side of bridge on the north side of the road. Follow this trail to Paint Branch, and continue south (downstream) to the outcrops with micaceous gneiss and stream banks that have abundant orange feldspar and micaceous gneiss.

Rockhounding

This site is located on the downstream side of the bridge that crosses Paint Branch just southeast of US 29. The road over Paint Branch is Old Columbia Pike, and automobile traffic is no longer allowed on this bridge. The rocks upstream of the bridge are mapped as part of the lower pelitic schist of the Glenarm Group, while the rocks downstream are mapped as part of the boulder gneiss of the Glenarm Group. The main difference between these two groups, not surprisingly, is that the former is primarily schist, and the latter is primarily gneiss.

This feldspar likely represents a section of feldspar-rich pegmatite that formed in the gneissic bedrock.

Outcrops are well exposed along the stream south of the bridge. The gneissic outcrops have abundant muscovite, but surprisingly did not have any garnet. The muscovite was generally fine-grained and not especially coarse. On the return trip upstream, we looked in the wide banks of rocks that formed near minor stream bends. These areas had some coarser mica schist rocks and numerous large pieces of orange feldspar. The large pieces of feldspar had to be broken to expose fresh surfaces, and the cleavages were often very sharp and strongly reflected sunlight. The key was to look for large pieces that were light orange and had a rough crystal outline consistent with feldspar, and to ignore rounded rocks that were often just sandstone or fine-grained granite.

Parking in this area is prohibited after sunset, and you must make sure that you park in the street and not at any of the nearby apartment complexes. It is best to visit early in the day so you get enough sunlight and avoid potential traffic tickets, towing, or other issues that may be present at this site. This is one of the most scenic and accessible stream canyons in the Washington, DC, area, and it makes an excellent morning field trip before spending the rest of the day in DC or other tourist areas.

References: Cleaves et al., 1968; Bernstein, 1980

76. Northwest Branch Tributary Garnet and Tourmaline

This tributary to Northwest Branch has garnet, and tourmaline-bearing mica schist can be found on the hillside on the north side of the stream.

See map page 250.

County: Montgomery

Site type: Loose rocks and outcrops along creek bed and hillside

Land status: Montgomery County Department of Parks and adjacent land

Material: Garnet and tourmaline

Host rock: Lower pelitic schist of the Glenarm series

Difficulty: Easy

Family-friendly: Yes

Tools needed: Hammer

Special concerns: Limited parking

Special attractions: Washington, DC

GPS parking: 39°03'24"N / 77°00'48"W

GPS pegmatite outcrop: 39°03'22"N / 77°00'40"W
GPS bridge over tributary: 39°03'24"N / 77°00'48"W
GPS tourmaline schist: 39°02'53"N / 77°00'40"W
Topographic quadrangle: Kensington, MD
Finding the site: Since this site is in a Montgomery County park, I assume there are several other places to park in the area for accessing the site, so you do not have to limit yourself to this parking area, which is very small. When visiting this site, I generally park on Remington Road, as this parking spot is next to the former Kensington Mine and the hike to the tributary passes a pegmatite outcrop.
To get to this parking area, head west on I-495 West and take exit 129 for MD 193 West. Turn right onto MD 193 West and continue 1.8 miles. Turn right (north) onto Arcola Avenue, go 0.8 mile, and turn right onto Kemp Mill Road. Continue 0.7 mile and turn right (east) onto Stonington Road. Go 0.5 mile and turn left (northeast) to stay on Stonington Road. Go 0.3 mile to the intersection of Stonington and Remington Roads. At this intersection, park on Remington Road next to a large grove of bamboo. A trail to Northwest Branch is adjacent to the west side of the bamboo grove. Follow this to the Northwest Branch of the Anacostia River, and hike approximately 1.25 miles to the bridge that crosses the tributary. Hike up the tributary approximately 1,500 feet to the tourmaline schist in the hills on the north side of the tributary.

Rockhounding

The parking area is across the street from a reported stockpile of mica from the Kensington Mine, which operated from 1882 to about the end of World War I. The stockpile is at the southwest corner of the intersection of Stonington and Remington Roads. Mica pieces can be found adjacent to the road along the drainage, but the stockpile is on private property and is heavily overgrown. The Kensington Mine was reportedly in a strip of county-owned land that has now been filled. It has been described as an obliterated locality, but in the early 1970s collectors were still finding beryl, garnet, apatite, and mica in the former dumps. Since the area is so heavily overgrown, though, I could not find any of the dumps or other indications of the mine. It might be advisable to return in late fall or early spring when the vegetative cover is least.

Although little remains of the Kensington Mine, you can hike to Northwest Branch and continue south to many garnet-bearing outcrops with some pegmatites. The first outcrop that you will reach on the west side of the trail has a prominent pegmatite dike with large masses of orange feldspar and some mica.

The black tourmaline is generally small and elongated roughly parallel to the foliation of the schist.

Farther south on the trail are additional outcrops with garnet and mica schist. When you reach a small wooden bridge, turn west and hike up this small tributary. There are several large rocks with garnet in the stream. The tributary has several large boulders that have been placed to stabilize the banks, but these are generally not mineralized. There are also many sewer manholes in the area, indicating that the stream area has been excavated and turned over many times. This also sometimes results in additional bedrock pieces being brought to the surface.

The extent of the park boundary is not marked in the area, so it is possible that you may be crossing into non-park land as you head west. Approximately 1,500 feet up the tributary, you can see some gray rocks on the north side of the hill. These are schists with long prismatic crystals of black tourmaline, which is often known as schorl. The black contrasts nicely with the silvery mica of the schist, and these are some interesting pieces. This area would also be very interesting to visit in late fall or early spring when the vegetation and the mosquitoes are at a minimum.

References: Cleaves et al., 1968; Bernstein, 1980

77. Travilah Serpentine Barrens

Parking is easy at this site as there is a very wide shoulder, and you can walk directly into the woods from here.

See map page 250.
County: Montgomery
Site type: Loose rocks in woods
Land status: Montgomery County Parks conservation area
Material: White to gray serpentine
Host rock: Serpentinite
Difficulty: Easy
Family-friendly: Yes
Tools needed: None
Special concerns: Conservation area; no collecting allowed
Special attractions: Washington, DC
GPS parking: 39°03'59"N / 77°13'40"W
Topographic quadrangle: Rockville, MD–VA

Finding the site: From I-270, take exit 8 and follow the signs for Shady Grove Road. Go southwest on Shady Grove Road for 3 miles, and the road turns into Piney Meetinghouse Road. Go 1.3 miles and park on the left (southeast) side of the road in a broad parking area, which is just past large power lines. The serpentine barrens that you can most easily access are in the woods northwest of the road and southwest of the power lines.

Rockhounding

The Travilah Serpentine Barrens are a 256-acre conservation park that is roughly bisected by a large power line. The Hunting Hill quarry, which is a large aggregate quarry, is just northeast of the park and is a well-known locality for serpentine group minerals, but it is not accessible without permission. The access to the serpentine barrens described here is relatively easy to reach, but it does not have any obvious trails, and you are limited to seeing the loose rocks and few outcrops poking up through the leaf cover.

The rocks on the surface are generally weathered serpentine. I did not find any waxy or fibrous serpentine minerals, but did find some weathered

Serpentine rocks lie around the ground surface in the woods.

light gray-green pieces that were strongly foliated. These rocks have intricate crenulations perpendicular to the strike of the foliation, indicating that the rock had been tightly folded during metamorphism. The interiors were often white and the folds could be distinguished by very thin layers in the original rock, which had been oxidized to dark brown limonite. Since this is a conservation area, I assume that collecting is not allowed, but it is still an interesting area to visit. One benefit of the soils derived from serpentine is that they are not as heavily overgrown as many other areas in Maryland, so walking through these woods can be considered rather pleasant since you are not constantly cutting through briars.

References: Cleaves et al., 1968; Bernstein, 1980

78. Great Falls of the Potomac

The gneissic rocks have prominent north–south trending joints, and the river flow is largely controlled along these pathways on Olmsted Island.

See map page 250.
County: Montgomery
Site type: Waterfalls and rapids through gneiss
Land status: Great Falls National Park
Material: Gneissic bedrock
Host rock: Late Precambrian metagraywacke of the Glenarm series
Difficulty: Easy
Family-friendly: Yes
Tools needed: None
Special concerns: No collecting allowed, viewing only
Special attractions: Canal boat rides on the Chesapeake & Ohio Canal
GPS parking: 39°00'10"N / 77°14'48"W
GPS Falls overlook: 38°59'48"N / 77°15'07"W
Topographic quadrangle: Vienna, VA–MD

Finding the site: From I-495 South, take exit 41 and merge onto Clara Barton Parkway. Go 1.5 miles, turn left onto MacArthur Boulevard, and go 3.4 miles. At the traffic circle, take the first exit as you enter the park. Park in the parking area and walk south on the canal path to the trail and bridges that cross the river to the Great Falls overlook.

Rockhounding

While this is not a site for collecting rocks, it is a site that must be seen when you are in the Washington, DC, area. The Great Falls of the Potomac is considered by many to be the most impressive natural feature in the region. The Potomac is usually a wide, flat river, but as it approaches the Fall Line, the river narrows and picks up speed. It narrows from nearly 1,000 feet, just above the falls, to between 60 and 100 feet wide as it rushes through Mather Gorge, a short distance below the falls. The river cuts deeply into the metamorphic bedrock and forms a series of steep rapids and waterfalls. The falls consist of cascading rapids and several 20-foot waterfalls, with a total 76-foot drop in

The Great Falls of the Potomac are one of the best expressions of the Fall Line in the eastern United States, and were a huge obstacle to early traders that used the Potomac for shipping goods by boat.

elevation in less than a mile. The Great Falls of the Potomac display the steepest and most impressive Fall Line rapids of the eastern rivers.

The rocks are mapped as late Precambrian metagraywacke of the Glenarm series, which is interbedded with schist. This tough, erosion-resistant metamorphic rock is well jointed, and the river follows joint patterns. The Park Service has built an excellent series of bridges and wooden walkways to reach the falls overlook, and it is a very safe place to walk, provided you stay away from the edge in the steeper areas. The park has also largely preserved the natural character by restricting hikers from walking in the woods. This keeps the undergrowth from being trampled, and it looks much more intact than similar woods that allow hikers. However, the preservation is only temporary, as fifty- and hundred-year floods eventually wipe out the soil and plants, and the cycle begins again.

Reference: Cleaves et al., 1968

REFERENCES CITED

Barwick, A. R. 1951. "Vivianite Concretions in the Aquia Formation (Middle Eocene), Anne Arundel County, Maryland." *American Mineralogist* 36 (7-8): 629–30.

Beard, Robert. 2004. "A Capital Collecting Opportunity." *Rock & Gem* 34, no. 6 (June 2004).

———. 2008. "Maryland's Mineral Hill Mine." *Rock & Gem* 38, no. 3 (March 2008).

Bell, Hugh S. 1940. "Armored Mud Balls: Their Origin, Properties, and Role in Sedimentation." *The Journal of Geology* 48, no. 1: 1–31.

Betts, John. 2009. "The Minerals of New York City." *Rocks & Minerals* 84, no. 3.

Bernstein, Lawrence R. 1980. *Minerals of the Washington, D.C. Area.* Maryland Geological Survey Educational Series No. 5.

Brezinski, David K. 1989. *Geology of the Sideling Hill Road Cut.* Maryland Geological Survey Pamphlet Series. Revised 1994.

Brodie, Peter Bellinger. 1858. "Geology Considered with Reference to Its Utility and Practical Effects." *The Geologist: A Popular Illustrated Monthly Magazine of Geology.*

Burns, Jasper. 1991. *Fossil Collecting in the Mid-Atlantic States.* Baltimore, MD: John Hopkins University Press.

Cleaves, E. T., J. Edwards Jr., and J. D. Glaser. 1968. *Geologic Map of Maryland.* Maryland Geological Survey, scale 1:250,000.

Crowley, W. P. 1976. *The Geology of the Crystalline Rocks Near Baltimore and Its Bearing on the Evolution of the Eastern Maryland Piedmont.* Maryland Geological Survey Report of Investigations No. 27, 39 pp.

Crowley, W. P., J. Reinhardt, and E. T. Cleaves. 1976. *Geologic Map of Baltimore County and City.* Maryland Geological Survey.

Day, William H. n.d. *Iron Mining at Newark, Delaware 1703–1910.* Chestnut Hill Iron Pit Preservation flyer.

Drake, Avery A. 1993. *The Soldiers Delight Ultramafite in the Maryland Piedmont.* US Geological Survey Bulletin 2076, AI–Al3.

Eckert, Allan W. 2000. *Earth Treasures Volume 1: The Northeastern Quadrant.* Lincoln, NE: iUniverse.com.

Edwards, Jonathon Jr. 1987. "Baltimore Gneiss and the Glenarm Supergroup, Northeast of Baltimore, Maryland," in *Geological Society of America Centennial Field Guide, Northeastern Section.*

Faill, Roger. 1991. *White Clay Creek Preserve, Chester County, Pennsylvania, New Castle County, Delaware: A Scenic Valley and the Arc Corner.* Pennsylvania Geological Survey, Pennsylvania/Delaware Trail of Geology Park Guide 20.

Free Lance Star (Fredericksburg, VA). 1992. Vol. 108, no. 158 (July 6), C-1.

Frye, Keith. 1986. *Roadside Geology of Virginia.* Missoula, MT: Mountain Press Publishing Company.

Geikie, Sir Archibald. 1858. *The Story of a Boulder; or, Gleanings from the Notebook of a Field Geologist.*

Glaser, John D. 1979. *Collecting Fossils in Maryland*. Maryland Geological Survey Educational Series No. 4. Revised 1995.

Hansen, Jess. 2013. *Smyrna, Clayton, and Woodland Beach*. Charleston, SC: Arcadia Publishing.

Heintzelman, Patricia, and Charles Snell. 1974. National Register of Historic Places Inventory-Nomination: New Castle, and accompanying 20 photos, from 1967 to 1974. National Park Service.

Heyl, A., and N. Pearre. 1965. *Copper, Zinc, Lead, Iron Cobalt and Barite Deposits of the Piedmont Upland in Maryland*. Maryland Geological Survey Bulletin 28, 72 pp.

Holly, David C. 1987. *Tolchester: The Delaware Connection and Tolchester the Golden Years, Steamboats on the Chesapeake*. Centreville, MD: Tidewater Publishers.

———. 1994. *Chesapeake Steamboats: Vanished Fleet*. Centreville, MD: Tidewater Publishers.

Jones, J. L., C. K. Scharnberger, M. A. Schlegel, and D. C. Robinson. 2006. "A Tour of the Peach Bottom Slate—Once the Best Building Slate in the World," in *Excursions in Geology and History: Field Trips in the Middle Atlantic States, Geological Society of America Field Guide* 8.

Lang, Helen M. 1996. "Pressure-Temperature Reaction History of Meta-pelitic Rocks from the Maryland Piedmont on the Basis of Correlated Garnet Zoning and Plagioclase-Inclusion Composition." *American Mineralogist* 81: 1,460–75.

Lauginiger, E. M. 1988. *Cretaceous Fossils from the Chesapeake and Delaware Canal: A Guide for Students and Collectors*. Delaware Geological Survey Special Publication 18.

Kranz, P. M. 1989. *Dinosaurs in Maryland*. Maryland Geological Survey Educational Series 6, 34 pp.

Kuff, Karen R., and J. R.V. Brooks. 1985. *The Building Stones of Maryland*. Maryland Geological Survey, 2 pp.

LaMotte, Richard. 2004. *Pure Sea Glass*. Chestertown, MD: Sea Glass Publishing.

Lynch, Peter. 2014. BrainyQuote.com, Xplore Inc. Accessed September 28, 2014. http://www.brainyquote.com/quotes/quotes/p/peterlynch173397.html.

Mackay, Bryan. 1995. *Hiking, Cycling, and Canoeing in Maryland: A Family Guide*. Baltimore, MD: Johns Hopkins University Press.

Maryland Historic Trust. 1984. Betterton Historic District, June 7, 1984, Inventory No. K-601, Betterton, Kent County.

Maryland State Archives. n.d. Historic American Buildings Survey K-317, Tolchester Beach Amusement Park.

McLennen, J. D. 1971. *Miocene Sharks Teeth of Calvert County*. Maryland Geological Survey pamphlet.

Means, John. 2010. *Roadside Geology of Maryland, Delaware, and Washington, D.C.* Missoula, MT: Mountain Press Publishing Company.

Moore, Herbert C. 1994. "A Brief History of the Copper Mine at Bare Hills, Maryland." *Matrix: A Journal of the History of Minerals* 3, nos. 4 and 5 (Fall).

Newcomb, Sally. 1994. "A History of Chromite and Copper in Maryland: The Tyson Years." *Matrix: A Journal of the History of Minerals* 3, nos. 4 and 5 (Fall).

Norden, Arnold. 2006. "The Cumberland Bone Cave: A Window into Maryland's Past." *The Maryland Natural Resource* (magazine of Maryland Department of Natural Resources), Fall.

Ostrander, C. W., and W. E. Price. 1940. *Minerals of Maryland*. Natural History Society of Maryland, 92 pp.

Parish, Preston. 1971. Catoctin Furnace, National Historic District National Register of Historic Places Nomination Form, F-6-45, Maryland State Archives.

Pearre, N. C., and A.V. Heyl Jr. 1960. *Chromite and Other Mineral Deposits in Serpentine Rocks of the Piedmont Upland, Maryland, Pennsylvania, and Delaware.* US Geological Survey Bulletin 1082-K.

Pickett, T. E., and N. Spoljaric. 1971. *Geology of the Middletown-Odessa Area, Delaware.* Delaware Geological Survey Geologic Map 2, scale 1:24,000.

Pickett, T. E., N. Spoljaric, and R. R. Jordan. 1976. *Generalized Geologic Map of Delaware.* Delaware Geological Survey Special Publication 9.

Purdum, William D. 1940. *The History of the Marble Quarries in Baltimore County, Maryland.* Records of Phi Mu, Special Collections, University of Maryland Libraries.

Ramsey, K. W. 2003. *Geology of the Lewes and Cape Henlopen Quadrangles, Delaware.* Delaware Geological Survey Geologic Map 12, scale 1:24,000.

———. 2005. *Geologic Map of New Castle County, Delaware.* Delaware Geological Survey Geologic Map 13, scale 1:100,000.

Reger, James P., and Emery T. Cleaves. 2008. *Physiographic Map of Maryland.* Maryland Geological Survey Open File Report 08-03-01.

Reger, James P., and Robert D. Conkwright. 2005. *Construction Information about the Sideling Hill Road Cut & Exhibit Center.* Maryland Department of Natural Resources Fact Sheet 17.

Robbins, Eleanora I. 1991. *Age of Early Cretaceous Palynomorphs in the Muirkirk Clay Pit Fossil Locality, Prince George's County, Maryland.* US Geological Survey Open-File Report 91-613, 5 pp.

Schenck, W. S., M. O. Plank, and L. Srogi. 2000. *Bedrock Geologic Map of the Piedmont of Delaware and Adjacent Pennsylvania.* Delaware Geological Survey Geologic Map 10, scale 1:36,000.

Shattuck, G. B., et al. 1907. *St. Mary's County.* Maryland Geological Survey County Reports, 209 pp.

Short, Kenneth M. 1999. Maryland Historical Trust State Historical Sites Inventory Form, Elba Furnace, Survey No. CARR-1586.

Singewald, Joseph T. 1911. *The Iron Ores of Maryland Volume 9*; With an Account of the Iron Industry. Baltimore, MD: John Hopkins Press.

Smoot, J. P. 1989. *Fluvial and Lacustrine Facies of the Early Mesozoic Culpeper Basin, Virginia and Maryland, July 14, 1989.* Field Trip Guidebook T213 for the 28th International Geological Congress, Washington, DC, American Geophysics Union, 15 pp.

Southwick, D. L., and J. P. Owens. 1968. *Geologic Map of Harford County.* Maryland Geological Survey County Geologic Map Series, scale 1:62,500.

Southworth, S., W. C. Burton, J. S. Schindler, and A. J. Froelich. 1999. *Digital Geologic Map of Loudoun County, Virginia.* US Geological Survey Open-File Report 99-150.

US Geological Survey. 1998. *Building Stones of Our Nation's Capital.* Reston, VA: US Geological Survey, 36 pp.

Usilton, Fred. 2010. *History of Kent County, Maryland, 1630–1916.* Charleston, SC: Nabu Press.

Virginia Division of Mineral Resources. 2003. *Digital Representation of the 1993 Geologic Map of Virginia.* Virginia Division of Mineral Resources Publication 174, compact disc.

Vokes, Harold E. 1957. *Miocene Fossils of Maryland.* Maryland Geological Survey Bulletin 20.

Ward, Lauck W., and Blake W. Blackwelder. 1980. *Stratigraphic Revision of Upper Miocene and Lower Pliocene Beds of the Chesapeake Group, Middle Atlantic Coastal Plain.* USGS Bulletin 1482-D.

Ward, R. F. 1959. "Petrology and Metamorphism of the Wilmington Complex, Delaware, Pennsylvania, and Maryland." *Geological Society of America Bulletin* 70: 1,425–58.

Woodruff, K. D., and A. M. Thompson. 1972. *Geology of the Newark Area, Delaware.* Delaware Geological Survey Map 3, scale 1:24,000.

———. 1975. *Geology of the Wilmington Area, Delaware.* Delaware Geological Survey Geologic Map 4, scale 1:24,000.

SITE INDEX

Washington, DC Metropolitan Area

ABOUT THE AUTHOR

Robert Beard is a geologist and has collected rocks for over thirty years. He received his BA in geology, with a minor in mathematics, from California State University, Chico in 1983 and his MS in geology from the University of New Mexico in 1987. He is a licensed professional geologist in Pennsylvania and works in the environmental consulting industry. He has collected rocks throughout much of the United States, the Caribbean, and parts of Europe. He is a contributing editor to *Rock & Gem* magazine and has written for *Rock & Gem* since 1993. His most recent books for FalconGuides include *Rockhounding Pennsylvania and New Jersey*, published in 2013, and *Rockhounding New York*, published in 2014. He currently lives in Harrisburg, Pennsylvania, with his wife, Rosalina, son Daniel, daughter Roberta, Nema the Chihuahua, and Lennon the Norwegian forest cat.

Credit: Rosalina Beard